POLICY AND PRACTICE IN HEALTH AND SOCIAL CARE

NUMBER ONE

Private and Public Protection: Civil Mental Health Legislation

POLICY AND PRACTICE IN HEALTH AND SOCIAL CARE

1: Jacqueline Atkinson, *Private and Public Protection: Civil Mental Health Legislation* (2006)

2: Charlotte Pearson (ed.), *Direct Payments and Personalisation of Care* (2006)

3: Joyce Cavaye, *Hidden Carers* (2006)

4: Mo McPhail (ed.), *Service User and Carer Involvement: Beyond Good Intentions* (2007)

5: Anne Stafford, *Towards Integration: Services for Children and Young People on the Margins* (2008)

6: Alison Petch, *Health and Social Care: establishing a joint future* (2007)

7: Gillian McIntyre, *Learning Disability and Social Inclusion* (2007)

8: Ailsa Cook, *Dementia and Well Being: possibilities and challenge* (2007)

POLICY AND PRACTICE IN HEALTH AND SOCIAL CARE
SERIES EDITORS
JOYCE CAVAYE and ALISON PETCH

Private and Public Protection: Civil Mental Health Legislation

by

Jacqueline M Atkinson

*Senior Lecturer in Psychology,
Public Health and Health Policy,
The University of Glasgow*

DUNEDIN ACADEMIC PRESS
EDINBURGH

Published by
Dunedin Academic Press Ltd
Hudson House
8 Albany Street
Edinburgh EH1 3QB
Scotland

ISBN 10: 1 903765 61 7
ISBN 13: 978-1903-765-61-6
ISSN 1750-1407

British Library Cataloguing in Publication data
A catalogue record for this book is available from the British Library

Typeset by Makar Publishing Production
Printed and bound in Great Britain by Cromwell Press

Contents

Series Editors Introduction

A key challenge for the social justice system of a country is how it responds to those who experience mental ill health. Where is the balance struck between the interests of the individual and of the wider society; how for the individual are individual rights traded against the need for protection and management of risk?

With devolution, Scotland has provided a clear lead in terms of mental health legislation. The Adults with Incapacity (Scotland) Act 2000 was one of the earliest pieces of legislation to be passed by the new Parliament. This has been rapidly followed by a second major piece of mental health legislation, the Mental Health (Care and Treatment) (Scotland) Act 2003, implemented in October 2005, which provides the focus for this volume. Both England and Scotland set up committees to review their legislative response to those individuals where some formal intervention might be deemed necessary. The subsequent responses however have been divergent. In England the Richardson Committee was followed by a series of proposals for a new Mental Health Act which in the face of much opposition have now been withdrawn, to be replaced by proposed modifications to the existing legislation. In Scotland, meanwhile, the recommendations from the Millan Committee were rapidly transformed into legislation based on ten core principles.

This volume traces these divergent routes and explores key features of the new Scottish legislation. These include the requirement for a test of capacity and the introduction of the compulsory treatment order with the potential for it to be community-based; the creation of the Mental Health Tribunal for Scotland with the power at individual hearings to detain and discharge individuals; the introduction of a right to advocacy; the provision to make advance statements; and the designation of the role of 'named person'. It provides an excellent baseline against which to compare alternative legislative responses in other jurisdictions.

Dr Joyce Cavaye
Faculty of Health and Social Care, The Open University in Scotland, Edinburgh

Professor Alison Petch
Director, Research in Practice for Adults, *The Dartington Hall Trust, Totnes, Devon, U.K*

Acknowledgements

Over a number of years I have had long, informative, sometimes heated and often multiple conversations with people about aspects of mental health legislation. These have all contributed to my understanding and thus this book. There are too many to name, but I need to give particular thanks to:

Helen Garner, Lesley Patterson and Jacquie Reilly, research associates who have worked with me on various projects and all of whom have become good friends, and Jacquie in particular for reading and commenting on a draft of this book; Kathryn Berzins, Graeme Henderson and Willie Munro, postgraduate students, whose projects around legislation allowed for endless speculation and exchange of views; Denise Coia (former Chair, Royal College of Psychiatrists, Scottish Division); Roch Cantwell (consultant perinatal psychiatrist); Eileen Davie (President, Mental Health Tribunal for Scotland); Jenny Graydon (Chief Executive, Glasgow Association for Mental Health); Donny Lyon (Director, Mental Welfare Commission for Scotland); Hilary Patrick (lawyer), Susan Stuart (philosopher) and Mary Weir (Chief Executive, National Schizophrenia Fellowship (Scotland)): also to James Trueman of Anglia Ruskin University for tracking down an unpublished thesis for me; service users and members of various mental health projects for informal discussions; Marvin Swartz, Jeffrey Swanson and colleagues at Duke University, North Carolina; Debra Srebnik at Washington State University and John Dawson of the University of Otago, New Zealand.

By no means least I would like to thank Alison Petch, not only the series editor but also a colleague for many years, for giving me the opportunity to indulge my interest in mental health legislation and write this book.

Glossary of Abbreviations

1983 Act	Mental Health Act 1983
1984 Act	Mental Health (Scotland) Act 1984
1995 Act	Mental Health (Patients in the Community) Act 1995
ASW	approved social worker
AWI	Adults with Incapacity (Scotland) Act 2000
CB-CTO	community-based compulsory treatment order
CCO	community care order
CCT	compulsory community treatment (order)
CTO	compulsory treatment order
CPN	community psychiatric nurse
HUG	Highland Users Group
JLIP	Joint Local Implementation Plan
LOA	leave of absence
MHCT Act	Mental Health (Care and Treatment) (Scotland) Act 2003
MHO	mental health officer
MHRB	Mental Health Review Board (Victoria, Australia)
MHRT	Mental Health Review Tribunal
MHTS	Mental Health Tribunal for Scotland
MSP	Member of the Scottish Parliament
NHS	National Health Service
OPC	outpatient commitment (order)
SAMH	Scottish Association for Mental Health
SDO	supervised discharge order

Introduction

The Mental Health (Care and Treatment) (Scotland) Act 2003 (MHCT Act, or, unless otherwise stated, 'the Act') came into operation in October 2005 to broad support, concerns about particular areas and some considerable anxiety about how it would affect services. Based on ten principles, it seeks to protect patients, both by strengthening their rights and seeking to preserve autonomy, but also by ensuring that people who are at significant risk and unable to make a competent decision about their medical care receive treatment – something that can be seen as protecting the public as well as the patient. Although public risk is usually seen in terms of direct risk to individual safety, society has wider concerns, and caring for people unable to do so for themselves may contribute to wider benefits.

This book only deals with the civil aspects of the new Act, and even then there is not space to do justice to its entirety, so some broad areas have been chosen. The Act is put in the context in which it came into being. The introduction of the tribunal system is such a material change that it cannot be overlooked. The introduction of community-based compulsory treatment orders was one of the most controversial elements and requires consideration. Advance statements, which have been greeted with enthusiasm in some quarters and could radically support patient autonomy and participation, may not live up to their expectations. The role of relatives has changed significantly with the introduction of the named person. Lastly, there is the impact on services and concern about the development of a two-tier service. Running through all these is the application of the underlying principles. The Act is a brave attempt to balance the interests of individual patients and the wider society. Time will tell how well it succeeds.

Chapter 1

Review of Mental Health Legislation: A New Act for a New Century

Britain in the 1990s saw a number of changes in mental health policy and practice which would lead to an agreed need to reform the existing mental health laws. Past revisions of the laws has seen Scotland largely follow England and Wales,[1] Scottish law being a year later but with little difference. The devolution of Scotland and the reconvening of the Scottish Parliament in 1999 saw this pattern change. Scotland pursued its own agenda on reform, leading to a significantly different outcome in the two countries (at the time of writing). Scotland has new mental health legislation, the Mental Health (Care and Treatment) (Scotland) Act 2003 (MHCT Act) (Scottish Parliament, 2003; Scottish Executive, 2003, 2004a). England and Wales still have no Act and a Mental Health Bill there, despite being withdrawn and supposedly redrafted (Department of Health, 2002a, 2004), still has no popular support from either professionals or service users' groups, carer organisations and civil liberty groups (Kmietowicz, 2002; Moncrieff, 2003; McKenzie, 2005; Public Health News, 2005; Thornicroft and Szmukler, 2005). In February 2006 it appeared that the bill had been postponed until 'parliamentary time allows' (Dyer, 2006). On 23 March 2006 the Health Minister, Rosie Winterton, announced that 'shorter, streamlined' legislation which would amend the existing 1983 Act would now be the way forward and would replace the controversial draft bill, which was withdrawn (Smith, 2006). Although this received a cautious welcome there was still concern that the government had not entirely given up its plans (Easton, 2006; MacAttram, 2006; Politics.co.uk, 2006). The Department of Health published a series of briefing sheets on 2 May 2006 outlining key policy areas where changes are proposed. These are supervised community treatment; professional roles; nearest relative; definition of mental disorder; criteria for detention and the Mental Health Review Tribunal. It is unlikely that these will meet all the concerns already expressed.

Despite the organisation of the health service in England and Wales being somewhat different from that in Scotland, policies stemming from the NHS and Community Care Act 1990 were broadly similar. The move to community-based care provided a challenge for Mental Health Acts based predominately on treatment in hospital. The 'provider' market meant that voluntary organisations were able to become major service providers. These basic similarities make the later divergence of the two countries over the reform of the legislation interesting and provide a context for considering the changes brought about by the new Act in Scotland.

Political and media influences on reform of the legislation

From the start of the 1990s the English-based national press covered a number of what became high profile cases involving people with mental illness or psychopathic personality disorder (for example Christopher Clunis, who killed Jonathan Zito in December 1992) and violence to the public. To a lesser extent there were stories of neglect and harm to patients (for example Ben Silcock, who went into the lions' den at London Zoo in December 1992).

In Scotland the stories were fewer and, with the exception of the case of Noel Ruddle (who sought discharge from the State Hospital at Carstairs), generated less media coverage. This is partly because there will be fewer cases with a population a tenth of that of England and Wales, but it also reflects the different system of dealing with such incidents. In England there is a public inquiry and the publication of a report. The media covers major cases not only at the time of the incident and trial but again when the report is published. This may contribute to the sense of a high number of violent crimes. There was also an investigation into the management of services at Ashworth Hospital, resulting in a lack of confidence in the system (Fallon et al., 1999). There was no such inquiry into the State Hospital in Scotland.

In Scotland incidents were investigated by the Mental Welfare Commission for Scotland, with no public report. The resulting media coverage was consequently more low key and likely to occur as a major story only once.

The last 15 years or so have shown an apparent growing interest in the media reporting of mental health. As with almost every issue in this book, a balance has to be struck. Yes, there are problems with a media which focuses on negative messages and images, of violence and neglect. Set against this is the need to recognise that the press has both a right and a duty to report events of public interest.

The inescapable reality is that some people with mental illness are violent, some extremely violent, and some commit homicide. Politicians have a duty to respond to this appropriately and responsibly, as do clinicians. Others may choose to respond however they see fit, which may or may not be seen by others as responsible or appropriate. What is not appropriate, however, is to argue that the media should not report these events because they lead to discrimination. The issue is responsible reporting.

The political response in the UK

The publicity, in England, of both violence by and harm to patients may have contributed to the approach taken by politicians to contain what some apparently saw as a potentially dangerous political situation.

Virginia Bottomley, then Secretary of State for Health in the Conservative government, demonstrated an almost knee-jerk reaction to Mr Silcock's foray into the lions' enclosure and introduced the supervision register in England in 1994 (Atkinson, 1996) This was not welcomed by psychiatrists, who saw it as putting them in a Catch 22 situation (Caldicott, 1994). If they put someone on supervised discharge and there was an unfortunate event they would be blamed for not having hospitalised the person, but if there was no supervised discharge they would be accused of not having carried out an appropriate risk assessment. These arrangements were quickly transformed by a new law, the Mental Health (Patients in the Community) Act 1995, which introduced supervised discharge orders (SDOs) in England and Wales and community care orders (CCOs) in Scotland. Neither was greeted with wholehearted enthusiasm by psychiatrists or patients, and the use of CCOs was patchy (Atkinson et al., 2000). These orders are important, however, as they foreshadowed the introduction of compulsory treatment in the community, in both the Scottish Act and the English bill.

The new measures did not seem to be having the desired effect and the constant trickle of media stories was causing politicians some concern. The new Labour government at Westminster faced this head on and, in a series of statements, announced that community care was not working. In the foreword to the policy document on modernising mental health services, Frank Dobson, then Secretary of State for Health, stated:

> Care in the community has failed because, while it improved the treatment of many people ... it left too many walking the streets, often at risk to themselves and a nuisance to others. A small but significant minority have been a threat to others or themselves. (Department of Health, 1998a)

To this was added the concern that dangerous people with a mental disorder were not being 'treated' appropriately. In this case, 'treated' was used to include detention in hospital as well as treatment with medication and other interventions. Psychiatrists came under attack and not just from politicians. This was illustrated by the case of Clarence Morris, diagnosed with an untreatable personality disorder, who was jailed after stalking Perry Southall and then released after 27 months, despite psychiatrists predicting him as an ongoing risk to the public. The judge, Peter Fingret, said it was 'regrettable' that he could not send Morris to Rampton Special Hospital. The desire for psychiatrists to deal with problems like this, maybe because the law could not, was demonstrated by someone from the Suzy Lamplugh

Trust: 'The fundamental problem is that for someone to be sent to a psychiatric hospital they need to have a treatable illness' (Woodcock, 1998).

Patients were not immune from 'blame' either, and the new political ethos of responsibility hit them. In announcing the review of the legislation, the then Health Minister, Paul Boateng, said: 'with our safety-plus approach, the law must make it clear that non-compliance with agreed treatment programmes is not an option' (Department of Health, 1998b)

There were no similar outbursts in Scotland from the newly elected MSPs (Members of the Scottish Parliament) apart from in relation to the release of Noel Ruddle. This loophole in the law was quickly closed by the first law of the new Scottish Parliament, the Mental Health (Public Safety and Appeals) (Scotland) Act 1999 (Scottish Parliament, 1999).

The reform process

Along with this media interest policy developments continued in both countries, with modernising agendas and new service frameworks (Department of Health, 1999a, Scottish Office 1997). The emphasis continued to be on the development of community-based services, with added agendas of not just reducing mental ill health but promoting positive mental health and reducing stigma. These latter programmes were particularly supported in Scotland by the Scottish Executive.

The Mental Health Acts (the Mental Health Act 1983 in England and Wales and the Mental Health (Scotland) Act 1984 in Scotland) were moderate revamps of the two previous Acts (1959 in England and Wales and 1960 in Scotland). They were still firmly based in a hospital-based system of care and treatment. Not all saw the need for change, nor the way ahead as clear. A conference in Edinburgh, 'The Mental Health (Scotland) Act: Consensus for Change', in December 1995 was organised by the Law Society of Scotland, the Royal College of Psychiatrists, Scottish Division and the Scottish Association for Mental Health (SAMH). This was in response to a groundswell of feeling in support of change and was a fitting rebuttal of a statement by Lord Fraser of Carmyllie (Minister of State at the Scottish Office) in the House of Lords on 16 March 1995:

> I acknowledge the case for considering whether the Acts [of England and Wales and Scotland] still reflect current practice. But there is no clear evidence at present, I believe, to conclude that they fail to meet present day needs and that there is not, as yet, any emerging consensus about how the position might change. (cited in conference programme)

Three hundred and five registered delegates (including academics, advocacy workers, carers, clinicians, lawyers, NHS and local authority managers, police, service users, sheriffs, social workers and people from voluntary organisations) from across Scotland combined to provide evidence that there was an 'emerging consensus' that change was needed, but not about the way forward. The pronouncements of politicians in England promoting a public safety approach led to the impetus for change dying somewhat. There was concern that a new Act could be more restrictive than the current one.

Then, in 1997, Scotland achieved devolution. Without this there might be no new Scottish Act. The Scottish Parliament came into being with a promise to pursue social justice and inclusiveness. In setting a new legislative agenda from scratch the Parliament was able to spend time on what some might otherwise have seen as minority issues. An early benefit of this was the Adults with Incapacity (Scotland) Act 2000 (AWI) (Scottish Parliament, 2000). The way was clear for a major revision of the legislation; to move its emphasis into line with predominately community-based service delivery and to reconsider the rights of patients: in short, to provide a modern Mental Health Act fit for the new millennium.

Committees of review were set up in both countries. The first was in England, announced by Frank Dobson in July 1998 and set up in October 1998. Chaired by Professor Genevra Richardson, Professor of Law at London University, it had the remit:

> To advise Ministers on the degree to which current legislation needs updating to support effective delivery of modern patterns of clinical and social care for people with mental disorder and to ensure that there is a proper balance between safety (both of individuals and the wider community) and the rights of individual patients. (Department of Health, 1999b, p. 127)

This 'balance' between public safety, individual rights and government policy was further emphasised by Paul Boateng, then Under-Secretary of State at the Department of Health, when introducing the Committee:

> Review of the Mental Health Act is long overdue ... it now reflects a bygone age ... It must also support the robust policies we are putting in place to ensure that services are safe, sound and supportive and that a proper balance is struck between the rights of individuals and the interests of the wider public on the few occasions when these can sometimes seem to conflict. (Department of Health, 1999b)

The Richardson Committee was to report to Parliament by April 1999, later extended to July 1999.

In Scotland the review committee was not established until February 1999. It was chaired by the Rt Hon. Bruce Millan, former European Commissioner and Secretary of State for Scotland in the Callaghan government:

an elder statesman of Scottish politics. He thus had good insight into how to negotiate potential political awkwardness. The remit of the committee was less restrictive than that of the Richardson Committee:

> In the light of developments in the treatment and care of persons with mental disorder, to review the Mental Health (Scotland) Act 1984, taking account of issues relating to the rights of patients, their families and the public interest. (Scottish Executive, 2001a, p. xi)

There was no overt political steer from the then Minister for Health, Sam Galbraith, as there was from Boateng. The committee also had longer to carry out its review, not reporting to the Scottish Parliament until January 2001.

Partly because of the time-frame, the Millan Committee was able to consult more widely, but from the outset it appeared that the review would be more inclusive than in England, with a wider range of people on the committee. In particular, the Scottish committee had two service users and two members of voluntary organisations, while the Richardson Committee had none. Although both had a carer, the carer on the Richardson Committee was also a GP and primary care lead for West Midlands Partnership in Mental Health.

Both committees produced consultation documents. Richardson produced *Key Themes* (sent to 220 groups/individuals) and the draft report (sent to the 250 who replied to the first consultation). Millan produced a consultation document, which was distributed widely across Scotland to over 1,000 groups or individuals, and a second consultation document sent to over 700. A shortened consultation document was sent to 1,000 users and carers, and a version produced specifically for people with a learning disability was sent to 600 people or organisations (Henderson, 2003).

The different time-frames meant that the Scottish review could take in more meetings and events. The Richardson Committee met, in full, on eight occasions (totalling 13 days), with subgroups meeting 15 times. Millan was able to meet, in full, 24 times (totalling 26 days), with subgroups meeting 41 times. To aid deliberations Richardson commissioned 10 papers, and held two international events (telephone seminars) and three other seminars. Millan commissioned two papers, held three events for users and carers and three whole-day seminars. Meetings were held with a wide range of stakeholder groups by both committees, and both made visits – Richardson 13 and Millan 37 (Henderson, 2003).

It could be argued that the Millan consultation was more inclusive and comprehensive than Richardson was. It was not only time that hampered Richardson. Her committee did not review the law relating to mentally disordered offenders 'given the uncertainty concerning the precise nature of the government's proposals in respect to severe personality disorder' (Henderson, 2003, p. 15). It also acknowledged that further consultation was required. The words of the Law Society of Scotland are testimony to the thoroughness of Millan:

> By the best standards of international work on mental health issues – which is basically three-cornered and concerns a balance of the rights of the patient, the needs of clinical effectiveness and the interests of society – the Millan committee's work is outstanding. (Adrian Ward, Law Society of Scotland, in Scottish Parliament, 2002f, col. 3244)

There were many similarities in the reports presented to their respective governments; not least the emphasis on underlying principles and the introduction of community-based compulsory treatment and mental health tribunals.

Although both reports were greeted by professionals and service users as being broadly fair and progressive (even if not every proposal was welcomed by all groups), it was at this point that the fate of the reforms in England and Wales and Scotland diverged sharply.

The Scottish Parliament received the Millan Report warmly, producing its policy document, *Renewing Mental Health Law* (Scottish Executive, 2001b). The foreword, signed by the then Minister for Health and Community Care, Susan Deacon, announced that the Scottish Parliament would 'implement the great majority of the Report's recommendations' (p. iii), within the context of the modernisation of services and the protection of the individual's rights. Public safety does make an appearance, with the statement that a Criminal Justice Bill would be introduced to protect public safety.

The Mental Health Bill (Scottish Parliament, 2002a) was published on 16 September 2002, following a draft bill published in June, and again it broadly followed the Millan Committee report, a point acknowledged by Millan.

> I am pleased about the bill as it stands. It has followed, sometimes in remarkable detail, the recommendations that my committee made. I think the bill will make very good legislation. (Rt Hon. Bruce Millan, in Scottish Parliament, 2002b, col. 3076)

It should be noted that this and other comments reflect the civil aspects of the bill. Modifications to the report in relation to mentally disordered offenders were more extensive: this part of the bill was scrutinised by the Justice Committee, not the Health and Community Care Committee, and is not discussed further in this book.

The responses were mixed but the bill was broadly welcomed by most, although areas of concern existed (Scottish Association for Mental Health, 2002). Comments made to the Health and Community Care Committee during Stage 1 of the progress of the bill reflect the variety of views (Scottish Parliament, 2002b–g).

> We are broadly happy with the bill. (Dr Jim Dyer, Mental Welfare Commission for Scotland, in Scottish Parliament, 2002b, col. 3057)

> The Royal College of Psychiatrists strongly welcomes the Mental Health (Scotland) Bill. It is based on sound principles ... particularly those safeguarding patients' rights and increasing the flexibility to manage people who are detained. (Dr Denise Coia, Royal College of Psychiatrists, in Scottish Parliament, 2002b, col. 3093)

> In general I believe that the bill has the potential to become a very good mental heath act. (David Hewitson, British Association of Social Workers, in Scottish Parliament, 2002b, col. 3128)

The main concerns for many groups were the introduction of community-based compulsory treatment and issues around consent for ECT (electro-convulsive therapy) and neurosurgery for mental disorder (Scottish Parliament, 2002d).

There was some concern that the bill had been drafted quickly and there was a need to get it through the various stages before the Parliament went into 'legislative purdah' before the general election. This hasty drafting accounted, in part, for the 1,400 amendments considered at Stage 2 of the bill.

The bill was passed by the Scottish Parliament on 20 March and received Royal Assent on 25 April 2003. The Act was expected to be implemented in April 2005 but a series of problems, mainly surrounding resource issues, including the development of the Mental Health Tribunal for Scotland (MHTS) meant the implementation date was set back to October 2005.

At Westminster, however, it was a different story as the Richardson report was largely ignored in the subsequent Green Paper (Department of Health, 1999b), and White Paper, *Reforming the Mental Health Act 1983* (Department of Health and Home Office, 2000). The White Paper was notable for being presented in two parts. Part I, the new legal framework, covered the area on which the Richardson Committee reported, although rejected many of its recommendations. Part II, 'High Risk Patients', was not part of the Richardson Committee's remit and was based on a government paper, *Managing Dangerous People with Severe Personality Disorder* (Home Office/Department of Health, 1999)

The Mental Health Bill was published on 26 June 2002. The rejection by the government of its commissioned consultation to pursue its own political agenda of public safety was met with hostility ranging from concern to outrage (Brown, 2002; Leason, 2002a; Leason et al., 2002). The President of the Royal College of Psychiatrists wrote to all members: 'We believe the proposals are both ethically unacceptable and practically unworkable. They represent little more than a Public Order Bill dressed up as Mental Health legislation' (Shooter and Zigmond, 2002). The mental health tsar, Professor Louis Appleby, however, continued to support the bill (Leason, 2002b).

The Blair government had succeeded in doing what might previously have been thought inconceivable: uniting virtually all stakeholder groups, from the Royal College of Psychiatrists to voluntary organisations such as Mind, in their opposition to the bill. Their reasons may have been different but these could be argued about later. For now, they were going to defeat the bill.

The bill was eventually withdrawn and a revised bill presented to Parliament in September 2004 (Department of Health, 2004): this also met with little support (Gillen, 2004; Kinton, 2005; Law Society, 2005). A Joint Committee of the House of Lords and House of Commons was set up as a pre-legislative scrutiny committee to consider ten key themes in relation to the draft bill. It first met on 15 September 2004 and reported on 23 March 2005. During this period 450 written submissions were considered, oral evidence was taken from 124 witnesses, and visits were made to three hospitals, including Broadmoor (Scott-Moncrieff, 2005). The committee made 107 recommendations or conclusions (House of Lords and House of Commons Joint Committee on the Draft Mental Health Bill 2005).

Reviewing the report, Scott-Moncrieff (2005) concluded, among other things, that:

> The recommendations of the Scrutiny Committee bear a striking resemblance to the proposals and recommendations made to the Department of Health by the Expert Committee in 1999 and by interested parties engaged in the endless consultations since that time. (Scott-Moncrieff, 2005, p. 82)

She then suggests that the 'Government should seriously consider adopting the Scottish Act; lock, stock and barrel'. An interesting observation is the note that 'huge amounts of public money, time and energy' have essentially been wasted on this exercise and that this should be investigated by an appropriate 'financial watchdog'.

The government published its response to the joint committee's report in July 2005 (Department of Health, 2005). Although there was acceptance of some of Richardson's recommendations, the most controversial elements of the bill were retained, including the enforced detention and treatment of patients where there was no clear therapeutic benefit. The Law Society warned that the bill was 'unworkable, misconceived, and would violate fundamental human rights' (Dyer, 2005).

The principles underpinning the reviews

Both the Millan and Richardson Committees produced a list of principles which they believed should underpin any new legislation. This reflected an approach based on human rights law, one that is seen to support legislation based on clear principles and positive rights (Franks and Cobb, 2005). Those of the Millan Committee were:

- non-discrimination;
- equality;
- respect for diversity;
- reciprocity;
- informal care;
- participation;
- respect for carers;
- 'least restrictive alternative';
- benefit;
- child welfare.

The Richardson Committee missed the last two but included consensual care, effective communication and provision of information.

In Scotland all the principles appeared in the policy statement and there was some surprise that they did not appear on the face of the bill as such, where some had been lost. There was widespread agreement both with the principles and with reinstating them. This came from voluntary organisations and the relevant professional bodies:

> We support the general principles absolutely, but we share the disappointment that many have expressed ... about the way in which the principles appear in the bill. (Shona Barcus, Scottish Association of Mental Health, in Scottish Parliament, 2002d, col. 3155)

> We feel that it would be preferable for the principles to be included in the bill. That would set the context. (Dr David Love, British Medical Association, in Scottish Parliament, 2002c, col. 3019)

> We would be very pleased to see those principles clearly spelled out. We think that the Millan principles are excellent and should underpin the practice behind the legislation. (David Hewitson, British Association of Social Workers, in Scottish Parliament, 2002c, col. 3127)

The Committee itself supported the inclusion of the principles:

> I think that it was because of the committee's work that the principles were included in the Adults with Incapacity (Scotland) Act 2000. That may be a portent of things to come – who knows? (Margaret Smith MP, Convenor, Health and Community Care Committee, in Scottish Parliament, 2002b, col. 3061)

Malcolm Chisholm, Minister for Health and Community Care for Scotland accepted this, at least in part:

> I am keen to make further progress on including the principles in the bill ... There is a continuing dialogue with the draftsmen and lawyers on the issue. We must at least respect and listen to what they say about transcribing principles into something that has legal meaning and can be interpreted and enforced. (Malcolm Chisholm, Minister for Health and Community Care, in Scottish Parliament, 2002g, cols 3331–2)

The principles are given expression in the Act, although not as an introductory list. This might be the reason why, despite their being some slight changes, it is the list of 'Millan principles' which is most commonly referred to, even by the Scottish Executive in its post-Act publications. The principles apply to most people, in most circumstances, where they discharge functions under the Act. They are legally binding duties, and are thus more than simply good intentions. Section 4 gives the Mental Welfare Commission for Scotland a duty to promote best practice in relation to the principles: a testament to their importance.

In England and Wales, 97% of those who responded to the consultation were in favour of including the principles in the Act (Department of Health, 1999c), but despite this they disappeared from the Green and White Papers and most are not explicit in the Act. Although the subsequent bills of 2002 and 2004 did not really move from this position, the House of Lords and House of Commons Joint Committee on the Draft Mental Health Bill (2005) concluded, as had been the case in Scotland, that the principles should appear in the English and Welsh Bill.

In England and Wales the joint scrutiny committee had ten key themes to address, the first of which was 'Is the draft Mental Health Bill rooted in a set of unambiguous basic principles? Are these principles appropriate and desirable?' Thornicroft and Szmukler (2005) also considered this question. They did so by referring to the new Scottish Act, the Richardson Committee and five more national and international policy statements. They helpfully summarised in table form the principles they drew from all of these. They pointed to a number of problematic areas, concluding that the bill did not meet the key principles in these documents, apart from the support for advocacy. They were concerned that:

> such an underground law will undermine the aspirations of both users and providers of mental health services to act in accordance with fundamental principles such as dignity, autonomy, empowerment, access and non- discrimination. In this sense it may not only be without principles, but there is a danger that in some circumstances ... its use could become unprincipled. (Thornicroft and Szmukler, 2005, p. 247)

While not wanting to minimise the very real anxieties over the government's intent, other commentators sounded notes of caution on Thornicroft and Szmukler's position. Maden (2005) suggested that Thornicroft and Szmukler based their arguments on four 'contentious' principles: 'doctor knows best', 'risk to self and others are equivalent', 'the purpose of mental health legislation was to reduce stigma' and 'therapeutic benefit is always necessary to justify detention'.

Commenting from the perspective of Australia, Mullen (2005) was clear that he did not want to defend the draft bill, but nevertheless also highlighted the simplicity of Thornicroft and Szmukler's argument. He pointed to the government's wavering commitment to community care which contrasts so dramatically with their indecent enthusiasm for Multi-Agency Public Protection Arrangements (MAPPA) and for the Dangerous People with Severe Personality Disorder Initiative (DSPD) (Mullen, 2005, p. 248). The public, he suggested, were right to be concerned about safety and this cannot be ignored, although the bill as it stands is 'unlikely to advance the agenda of community safety'.

Although all the principles are important, possibly the ones which excited the most general interest were reciprocity and least restrictive alternative.

> We urge the committee to include a reference in the bill to the principle of the least restrictive alternative, because in the past 15 years psychiatry has reduced its beds and moved patients into the community ... Reciprocity is a vital principle, because it protects patients' autonomy. It is vital in preventing the misuse of psychiatry to control social problems. (Dr Denise Coia, Royal College of Psychiatrists, in Scottish Parliament, 2002b, cols 3093–4)

The definition of mental disorder

The new Act applies to people with a mental disorder, which is then defined as mental illness, learning disability and personality disorder. These are not defined further. Personality disorder is now a category in its own right, whereas it had been a sub-category of mental illness under the 1984 Act. This change may make it easier for people with personality disorder to be subject to the Act, particularly taken in context with the wider definition of medical treatment (section 329) which means they may be more likely to meet the treatability test.

The definition of mental disorder needs to be fairly wide because the Act puts duties on health boards and local authorities to provide services for such people. Other criteria are invoked (see next chapter) before someone can be detained and compulsorily treated. The definition of mental disorder and medical treatment are discussed in Volume 1 of the Code of Practice (Scottish Executive, 2005a).

Although the majority of people who come under the civil provisions for detention and compulsory treatment have a mental illness, provision must also be made for patients with learning disability and personality disorder.

Figures are difficult to obtain for each group as the Mental Welfare Commission does not give this information in its annual reports.

When the Scottish bill was published it did not seek to define mental disorder any further, nor did it offer any exclusions. It could be argued that exclusions are unnecessary because mental disorder is already defined as mental illness, learning disability and personality disorder, and anything which does not come under these headings is not a mental disorder. There was some concern from some groups about the inclusion of learning disability, and discussion around the appropriateness of including personality disorder. The Royal College of Psychiatrists supported explicit exclusion criteria (Scottish Parliament, 2002b–g).

Exclusions were reinstated into the Act and appear in section 328. They cover:

- sexual orientation;
- sexual deviancy;
- transsexualism;
- transvestism;
- dependence on, or use of, alcohol or drugs;
- behaviour that causes, or is likely to cause, harassment, alarm or distress to any other person;
- acting as no prudent person would act.

Given changeable social attitudes to some aspects of human behaviour, it was seen as important to give a clear signal that none of these behaviours or orientations are considered a mental disorder. Indeed, they cannot be used as a justification for securing compulsory treatment or detention without a change to the law. Any of these behaviours and orientations can co-exist with a mental disorder, but it is the mental disorder to which the Act applies. Alcohol and drug use in particular may exacerbate symptoms and behaviours which lead a person to being detained and/or compulsorily treated.

The Law Society gave a vivid example of the need for these exclusions in relation to the bill in England and Wales, which still does not have such exclusions and which maintains a very broad definition of mental disorder (Law Society, 2005). In their response to the draft bill they pointed out that nicotine dependency could, under the bill, result in someone being detained and compulsorily treated. Nicotine dependency is included in both ICD-10 and DSM-IV classification:[2] medical treatment is warranted, the dependency demonstrates serious neglect of the person's health or safety, the person continues to smoke, and treatment is available. They pointed out that the bill gave no discretion to clinicians over the use of compulsory treatment where criteria are met (a discretion which is available in the 1983 Act).

The criteria that are required, along with a mental disorder, before someone can be compulsorily treated or detained are covered in the next chapter. In developing the criteria for detention and compulsory treatment, or even in defining mental illness, there is always a balance to be found between being so wide that it covers too many people (and thus causes anxieties about civil liberties) and so narrow that many of the people who might benefit are excluded.

Mental health and mental incapacity legislation: complementary or confusing?

At the same time as the debate about the need to revise the mental health legislation, a separate, but linked, debate was going on regarding people with compromised capacity. Some people believed that to have two different pieces of legislation was unnecessary and would give rise to confusion. In Scotland the need for an 'Incapacity Act' had been debated for some time, with the Law Society for Scotland being heavily involved. With the reinstatement of the Scottish Parliament the possibility of this law was seen as coming a step nearer. There was an awareness that it might be prudent to revise the Mental Health Act 1984 at the same time as writing what would become the Adults with Incapacity (Scotland) Act 2000, but the incapacity legislation was considered too important to be held up further. The need to clarify the legal position for adults with incapacity in a number of important areas was seen as urgent and took priority, and the AWI became law just as the review of the Mental Health Act got underway.

At least having the AWI established in law meant the revision of the mental health legislation had a stable Act with which to work. This has not been the case in England and Wales, although the Mental Capacity Act there received Royal Assent on 7 April 2005. A comprehensive comparison of the two Acts in Scotland is given by Gordon (2004). Although it is expected that there will need to be a period of adjustment, the aims of the two Acts are seen as separate. The MHCT Act contains a form of incapacity criterion in its conditions for use: this helps in linking the two Acts and deciding which one is the most appropriate. This impaired decision-making ability criterion means that there should not be the need to 'move' people between the two Acts as they lose or gain capacity, which is a possibility envisaged in England and Wales (Law Society, 2005, Richardson, 2005). This is because the current draft Mental Health Bill there does not have a similar incapacity/impaired ability clause. Indeed, the Law Society went so far as to state its belief that the relationship between the two bills is so complex that in many cases it would be practically impossible to work out which of the two Acts should be used and which should not (Law Society, 2005, p. 73).

It is worth noting that the prelegislative scrutiny committee suggested that compulsory or non-consensual treatment should be dependent on impaired decision-making ability as a result of mental disorder (the same as in Scotland) (House of Lords and House of Commons Joint Committee on the Draft Mental Health Bill, 2005).

Notes

1. England and Wales have the same mental health legislation, the Mental Health Act 1983. For ease in the text they will be referred to as one country.
2. ICD-10 is the classification system for mental disorders most commonly used in Britain and Europe and DSM-IV is used in North America.

Chapter 2

Compulsory Treatment and Detention

The power to compel a person to receive treatment against their wishes is possibly the first thing that comes to mind when thinking about mental health legislation. It is a remarkable legislative power that can be used, depending on the person's perspective, as a liberal and humane way to treat people who would otherwise be left without treatment and largely disowned by society; or as a discriminatory and socially controlling power to manage people who do not fit in and of whom society does not approve. To say the reality lies somewhere in the middle is not necessarily to sit on the fence but to balance what the legislation allows professionals to do, with the way it is perceived by those who come under its powers.

The MHCT Act has made several major changes to detention and compulsory treatment. It changed the criteria for detention so that they include a form of capacity criterion and also a treatment or benefit test. It also replaced long-term detention with the compulsory treatment order (CTO), which can be either hospital- or community-based. Guides to emergency and short-term detention, and to CTOs for service users and carers, have been produced by the Scottish Executive (2005b, c).

Criteria for detention and compulsory treatment

The criteria for a CTO are set out in section 64(5). They are:

(a) that the patient has a mental disorder;

(b) that medical treatment which would be likely to

(i) prevent the mental disorder worsening, or

(ii) alleviate any of the symptoms, or effects, of the disorder

is available to the patient;

(c) that if the patient were not provided with such medical treatment there would be a significant risk

(i) to the health, safety or welfare of the patient, or

(ii) to the safety of any other person;

(d) that because of the mental disorder the patient's ability to make decisions about the provision of such medical treatment is significantly impaired;

(e) that the making of a compulsory treatment order in respect of the patient is necessary;

(f) where the Tribunal does not consider it necessary for the patient to be detained in hospital, such other conditions as may be specified in regulations.

It should be noted that the risk involved has to be significant. Risk to self has been extended from the 1984 Act to include welfare.

One aim of the new Act is to reduce the number of emergency detentions, making short-term detention the primary route to compulsory care. The first four months of the Act indicate that emergency detention is down by 60% but short-term detention has only gone up by 27% (Kappler, in press). It is too early to comment further on this and the reasons for it, but it may be that this aim will be achieved.

Possibly the most important change is the introduction, for the first time in a British Mental Health Act, of the need for the person to have reduced capacity. This applies to emergency and short-term detention as well as for a CTO. This is a significant step forward for patients' rights. Under the Mental Health Act 1984 a person who could competently refuse treatment could still be forced to comply with it. Under the new Act a person who can competently refuse treatment, for example medication or ECT, cannot be compelled to receive it. The wide definition of treatment, however, means that such a person may still be subject to detention. A person cannot refuse to be detained.

But what if someone who is at risk, either to themselves or to others, but who understands this risk and apparently has unimpaired ability to make decisions about treatment, decides to refuse treatment and take the risk of something 'bad' happening? Will they be allowed to do this? For example, a person has severe negative side effects from medication and decides they do not want to continue to take medication. When ill they are at significant risk of:

- attempting suicide;
- going 'walk-about': i.e. leaving home, living rough, neglecting to eat and personal safety;
- self-harm requiring treatment but short of life threatening;
- being exploited (or abused), which may affect their personal safety or health;
- minor aggressive outbursts to others;
- violence/aggression which could result in the person requiring treatment;
- killing someone.

It is quite possible that judgements about impaired decision-making ability will be influenced by the severity of the consequences of not detaining or treating for the individual as well as others. It can be argued that protecting a person's best interests is served in terms of not just stopping them harming themselves, but also stopping them harming others. This assumes that rational people do not want to harm others, and therefore that to prevent someone doing something they would not do if rational, and may deeply regret afterwards, is to protect their moral sensibilities and is thus in their best interest. For someone with a learning disability who has never had (and never will have) the capacity to understand and make these moral decisions for themselves, the norms of the majority society are being imposed. While this might be controversial in some areas, in this case, where such norms are supported by laws prohibiting injury to others, it may be the least restrictive alternative. On a more practical level, the more serious the harm to others the more likely it is that the person will be detained (under procedures for mentally disordered offenders) for a considerable period of time, possibly the rest of their life. Again, it is assumed that it is in the person's best interest to prevent such incarceration.

Much has been written about capacity or competence.[1] How capacity is best defined and measured, along with its relationship with informed consent, has been discussed in detail elsewhere (e.g. Grisso and Appelbaum, 1995, 1996; Grisso et al., 1995; Law Commission, 1995). As previously noted, this may cause some confusion with the AWI Act, but since the intention is that the Acts are there to do different things time will indicate how the Acts are used independently or jointly to manage people with compromised capacity.

A potential problem with the MHCT Act is how this impaired decision-making ability is to be assessed. It is not the same as a full capacity assessment – the person has not lost capacity as such, but does have an impairment, which may be judged at a lower threshold. Volume 2 of the Code of Practice gives some guidelines on impaired decision-making (Scottish Executive, 2005d), suggesting that factors taken into account could:

> involve consideration of the extent to which the person's mental disorder might adversely affect their ability to believe, understand and retain information concerning their care and treatment, to make decisions based on that information, and to communicate those decisions to others. (Scottish Executive, 2005d, p 14)

Nor does this have to affect anything other than the person's ability in respect of medical decisions. Furthermore, this impaired ability has to result from the mental disorder, but should not be seen as synonymous with mental disorder.

The thinking behind this would seem to be that the particular ways in which mental disorders affect the person's reasoning abilities have to be taken into account. Although the prime suspect here is the 'lack of insight' frequently noted in people with psychosis, notably schizophrenia, it is not restricted to this. Depression can cause people to underestimate the success of treatment because of negative, nihilistic or hopeless thinking. It may cause the person to believe that they do not deserve treatment because they are wicked or undeserving. Indeed the depression may cause them to believe that they deserve to suffer. In such cases the person is not choosing illness in any positive sense so much as denying their right to be any different, or well.

The Code of Practice contrasts impairment with incapacity, which 'broadly involves a disorder of the brain and cognition which implies actual impairment or deficits which prevent or disrupt the decision-making process' (Scottish Executive, 2005d, p. 16).

With anorexia nervosa the position is slightly different. Anorexia has been described as more than an illness; as 'a social phenomenon outside the legal or medical perspective' (Melamed et al., 2003). The Ana websites that have proliferated in the last few years testify to how this condition is understood by people with it, many of whom consider it a lifestyle choice. How this affects the person's capacity to make decisions about medical treatment is open to question.

Elsewhere it has been argued that although people with anorexia are able to make decisions about many aspects of their lives, they are not able to make decisions about their body weight, treatment and diet (Tan et al., 2003a, b, c). Melamed et al. (2003) described this as a single delusional disturbance, which justifies the use of detention and compulsory treatment.

The arguments for not compelling people to accept treatment are many, and include respecting the person's wishes. Although a person may choose illness over treatment, particularly where the treatment itself has considerable negative side-effects, this is a decision which is probably best made when it is not clouded by the illness. For this reason the MHCT Act introduces advance statements.

The consequences of not treating someone affect the individual, their family, services and the wider society. Mental illness carries with it a significant mortality rate. Anorexia has the highest mortality rate of all psychiatric disorders (Webster et al., 2003).

Community-based compulsory treatment

The debate around compulsory treatment in the community surfaced in Britain in the early 1990s, but had been around for longer elsewhere. These debates have been summarised elsewhere (Atkinson and Patterson, 2000; Gerbasi et al., 2000, Dawson et al., 2003). The Millan Committee was persuaded by the least restrictive alternative argument. Community-based compulsory treatment orders (CB-CTOs) were probably the most controversial change to compulsory treatment in the MHCT Act, although the phrase itself does not appear in the Act.

> We are concerned that the proposals in relation to community-based compulsory treatment orders might lead to an unintended increase in the use of compulsion. (Professor Kevin Woods, Scottish Association for Mental Health, in Scottish Parliament, 2002e, col. 3208)

> If a compulsory treatment order means that someone does not need to be in hospital and can live with friends, carrying out their usual activities but having a degree of control that may be a good option. However ... is it the first step towards treating people more forcibly, more paternalistically and in a more authoritarian manner in the community, where normally people would see themselves as free? ... That worries us. (Graham Morgan, Highland Users Group, in Scottish Parliament, 2002f, col. 3262)

There are a number of strands to the arguments both for and against the introduction of compulsory treatment in the community. Which strand comes to prominence depends on how the question is asked. For example:

- do people who are ill enough to need compulsory treatment have to be in hospital?
- is hospital the only appropriate place for compulsory treatment?
- if someone is well enough to stay in the community should they be required to accept compulsory treatment?
- is compulsory treatment in the community a response to a lack of hospital beds and a cost-cutting response to treating people?
- is compulsory treatment in the community a response to trying to keep people out of hospital as much as possible?

Some of the unease about CB-CTOs focused on service users' concerns that community psychiatric nurses (CPNs) would be in and out of their homes several times a day to check that they had taken their medication (Scottish Parliament, 2002d, f). This was a misunderstanding of what would happen in most cases. Patients on leave of absence (under the 1984 Act) were not usually checked up on in this way. Non-compliance with medication usually becomes apparent either through blood tests (where these are routine, e.g. for lithium, Clozapine) or because a person relapses.

Concerns about CB-CTOs being used as cost-cutting measures will be discussed in the final chapter.

Dawson (2005) pointed to five sets of issues surrounding compulsory community treatment (CCT) that are common to all legal jurisdictions: ethical, constitutional, political, legal and empirical. They may be condensed into two main areas, those to do with civil liberties and rights, and those to do with outcome, or the success of using CCT.

There would seem to be little doubt that when envisioned by the Millan

Committee the introduction of CB-CTOs was seen as an advance, a way of limiting the impact of compulsory treatment on the individual. By separating compulsory treatment from detention in hospital, Millan believed it was supporting the principle of least restrictive alternative. It was almost taken as axiomatic that:

- being in the community (even on compulsory treatment) was less restrictive (which probably includes concepts of being less stigmatising) than being in hospital; and
- patients would prefer to be at home than in hospital.

That the latter is not true for all patients has come as a surprise to some:

> For me, as for everybody else in the room, my home is my home. It is a place where I have fun with my nephews and nieces and to which, after a tough day at the office ... I can go home, put the music on and sit on the couch. The fact that I would be required to let health professionals and social workers into my home if I was put under compulsion disturbs me ... If compulsion were to extend to my home, it would become not my home but a house. That is one reason why I would hate to be put under such an order. (Maggie Keppie, Edinburgh Users Forum, in Scottish Parliament, 2002f, col. 3287)

She is later clear that, although she would find being in hospital less restrictive, this is a personal view and people should have choice.

Another user said:

> I would prefer not to be treated in the community. If people are ill enough to be sectioned they are ill enough to be in hospital. (Marcia Reid, Highland Users Group, in Scottish Parliament, 2002f, col. 3262)

Some expressed surprise at this position:

> I was surprised that some people might prefer to be treated compulsorily in hospital rather than at home. That came as a shock to me and I admit I was not prepared for it. (Professor David Owens, Royal Edinburgh Hospital, in Scottish Parliament, 2002f, col. 3262)

Although the introduction of CB-CTO was treated as an extension of current powers and a new departure for the legislation, in fact various forms of community compulsory treatment have been in existence for some time (Atkinson and Patterson, 2000; Atkinson et al., 2005). The Mental Health Acts of 1983 (England and Wales) and 1984 (Scotland) allowed for patients on a long-term detention order to be discharged into the community on leave of absence (LOA). Under this provision patients could be returned to hospital, if necessary, without the need to go through a formal detention procedure, although in practice this was not a common outcome (Atkinson et al., 1999). There was concern about the increasing use of LOA and the length of time some patients spent on leave of absence (Atkinson et al., 1998, 1999, 2002a). A challenge to the law in England resulted in LOA being curtailed at six months. With no such challenge in Scotland, LOA could be extended, annually, indefinitely. With the number of people on LOA increasing this was a cause of anxiety. The Mental Health (Patients in the Community) Act 1995 standardised the period a person could be on LOA in the two countries at 12 months.

As well as reducing the length of time for which LOA was available in Scotland, the 1995 Act also introduced community care orders (CCOs). To many this appeared a compromise. The orders allowed for a person to be compulsorily managed in the community, but not necessarily treated. There was no provision for compelling a patient to take medication, which led a number of psychiatrists to see little use for it, describing it as 'without teeth' (Atkinson et al., 1997). Despite this, some psychiatrists changed their minds about the usefulness of CCOs after experience of them (Atkinson et al., 2002b). Not all psychiatrists saw the lack of clear provision for compulsory medication, and it was clear that there was some economy of full disclosure: some patients clearly believed they had no choice but to accept medication (Atkinson et al., 2002c). From their introduction on 1 April 1996 until 31 December 1999, 45 CCOs were granted, the equivalent of one a month. Of these, 49% were judged by the psychiatrist as broadly successful. The psychiatrist judged 35% as unsuccessful, largely because of lack of compliance with medication (Atkinson et al., 2002b). The remainder were seen as making no difference.

One anxiety about compulsory community treatment was whether this is a response to lack of other appropriate resources. The implications of this will be discussed in the final chapter, but the content of local services, or other local characteristics, must always be borne in mind. In 1999 a national study was conducted in Scotland, covering 1 April 1996 to 31 December 1998, with 266 patients on either LOA or a CCO. There appeared to be no pattern of use relating to geographical characteristics (e.g. rural versus urban health boards) (Atkinson et al., 2004a). The range was from a high of 8.2 per 100,000 population in the Tayside Health Board area to a low of 2.9 per 100,000 in Ayrshire and Arran. It should be noted when considering these figures nationally that patients from Shetland and Orkney are transferred to Grampian Health Board (the site of the psychiatric hospital) for long-term orders and appear under the Grampian figures. During this period the Western Isles (with a population of less than 30,000) had no long-term orders.

The belief that community-based compulsory treatment would always be less restrictive than being in hospital was brought into question by the conditions placed on some people. The need to protect the privacy of individuals means that giving full details of orders is difficult, where this might identify a person. Suffice it to say that where an order requires a person to have someone live with them, not go out alone and be restricted where they go, the restrictions on their privacy, let alone their liberty, are considerable. Whether such an individual would have more privacy and small freedoms in hospital is open to debate. This is likely to be the case for some groups of behaviours more than others. Thus people whose management includes dealing with inappropriate sexual behaviour may be at much lower risk in hospital, where opportunities are less, than in the community and may thus have more day-to-day freedom in hospital than in the community.

In England and Wales the near equivalent of CCOs were supervised discharge orders (SDOs). These were also used in a patchy, less-than-consistent way. Between September 1988 and May 1999 a sample of 170 mental health trusts used 596 SDOs, the equivalent of 1.2 per 100,000 population (Pinfold et al., 2001; Hatfield et al., 2004). The number in each trust ranged from no orders to 32.

In both countries the use of guardianship is available under the Mental Health Acts for people who are, or have become incapacitated. Its use under the Mental Health Act in Scotland is not extensive, but was increasing during the 1990s, although there had been a general decline in its use since the early 1960s (following the previous revision of the Mental Health Act). In 2004–5 there were 1,042 guardianship orders in Scotland, giving a ratio of 7.8 per 100,000 of the population (Mental Welfare Commission, 2005a). It should be borne in mind that this was the third year of the AWI Act and its impact could be seen in the increasing number of private applications. Since the advent of the AWI it is likely that it would be more appropriate for most cases of guardianship for people with dementia and learning disability than the Mental Health Act.

The new CTO is designed to enable individualised plans to be made for the care and treatment of those patients who require compulsory treatment. This puts them in the slightly odd position of supporting an individual approach, which should include listening to the patient, including then in decisions and so forth, while at the same time forcing them to accept unwanted (even if their decision was impaired) treatment.

The compulsory treatment order

Applying to the Mental Health Tribunal for Scotland for a CTO has four stages. Broadly, these are:

- A medical examination of the patient is carried out by two medical practitioners and submitted to the mental health officer (MHO).
- The MHO must tell the patient, their named person and the Mental Welfare Commission that an application is being made.

- The MHO interviews the patient (unless impracticable) and writes a personal circumstances report.
- The MHO writes, in collaboration with the two doctors who provided medical reports and after consulting with service providers, a 'proposed care plan'. This is later followed by a 'social circumstances report' (SCR).

If the tribunal grants a CTO, the responsible medical officer then has to prepare the care plan, covering:

- proposed or prescribed medical treatment (which includes all forms of treatment, community care services and other services given to the patient);
- the objectives of such treatment;
- the compulsory measures granted by the tribunal;
- recorded matters granted by the tribunal;
- the date of the next mandatory review of the CTO.

Where a CTO specifies detention in hospital or residence at a specific place, there is authorisation to take the patient to that place within seven days.

A CTO is made for a period of six months and can be renewed for a further six months and then yearly after that. It is the provision for residence at a specified address that allows for the CTO to have a community base rather than a hospital base.

The proposed care plan lays out the addressed needs of the patient and it is these which the care plan, through the CTO, must address. The Act's definition of medical treatment is very wide and includes:

(a) nursing;

(b) care;

(c) psychological intervention;

(d) habilitation (including education, and training in work, social and independent living skills; and

(e) rehabilitation (read in accordance with (d) above (s. 329(1))

The Code of Practice spells this out as including pharmacological interventions, other physical interventions including ECT, and social interventions such as occupational therapy, along with psychological interventions (Scottish Executive, 2005a).

The conditions which could be imposed under a CTO are thus very extensive, and this is one of the things which has caused such consternation. The proposed care plan should include alternatives that have been considered, along with a risk assessment which should support the principle of least restrictive alternative. It should be noted, however, that not everything in a care plan may be compulsory. At the tribunal hearing the tribunal can vary the care plan, adding to or subtracting from it having listened to the views of all relevant people. This could be the patient and their named person and/or carer as well as a variety of service providers/professionals. The main focus in the debate has, probably inevitably, been medication and compelling a person to take unwanted medication while living in the community. A difficult Catch 22 situation arises here. The parts of the argument are, broadly:

- A person should not be compelled to take medication if they are able to live in the community.
- The person is only able to live successfully in the community if they take their medication.
- The person will only take their medication if compelled under the Mental Health Act. Subsidiary issues under this point are:
    - the person has indicated they will stop taking their medication if they have a choice;
    - the patient's past history indicates they will stop taking their medication when they feel better as they believe they do not need it (or variants on this).

These points give rise to different scenarios when the CTO might be imposed. Many people, including voluntary organisations and user groups, have argued that compulsory medication in the community should only be used when there is a proven history of stopping medication and consequent relapse. They have opposed it for people with a first episode of illness.

It could be argued that someone might need to go through the experience of stopping medication and relapsing to understand the process and learn to manage their illness. Conversely, experiencing a period of a CB-CTO may also be necessary for the person to make an informed choice (Saks, 2003).

The Royal College of Psychiatrists outlined how they saw CTOs being used:

> The debate is not about the number of in-patient beds. It is about people who relapse. The rate of relapse in the community is higher because people there do not take medication, they add alcohol and drugs to their systems and so relapse more quickly. We believe CTOs should be used to reduce the incidence of relapse, not as an alternative to acute in-patient admission. (Dr Denise Coia, Royal College of Psychiatrists, in Scottish Parliament, 2002e, col. 3221)

They also made comments specifically about community-based CTOs:

> I will make a point about community-based CTOs and patients relapsing. One of the major problems when people with chronic mental illness relapse and are taken into hospital, as opposed to staying in the community, is that they lose some of their self-

> esteem and self-confidence. That is important. They often slide socially because their friends do not want to know them. They can lose all such social contacts. They also slide economically. Their jobs are put on hold and they usually lose them. Such people move themselves completely out of normal life. The Royal College of Psychiatrists is pleased that the bill will give us the tools to treat and manage that group in the community so that some of this slide does not happen. (Dr Denise Coia, Royal College of Psychiatrists, in Scottish Parliament, 2002e, col. 3224).

This position was supported by the Association of Directors of Social Work (Scottish Executive, 2002c).

To address these issues means accepting that the risk assessment was such that simply leaving the person alone is not an option and that any intervention will have negative as well as positive impacts. The principles underpinning the Act should form the basis of making the decision. This in turn means balancing all the principles, not just using those that suit the particular argument.

Evidence in the use of compulsory community treatment

Behind all the concern is the question of whether CCT can 'work'. This in itself is a difficult question because 'work' can mean a variety of different things to different people in different contexts. The view of what works from the perspective of a treating psychiatrist may be very different from the patient's view. This covers not only what sort of outcomes or experiences are included as evidence, but whether it is even appropriate to consider CCT in this way. Compulsory treatment, whether in the community or not, is not an intervention as such but a means of delivering services or interventions to patients. It can thus be evaluated as a process and success, or otherwise, examined from the perspective of keeping patients in touch with services or receiving treatment. Success in a wider, clinical sense, including changes in behaviour, relapse and so forth will be dependent on the effectiveness of the interventions or treatment the person receives. Put crudely, CCT could be deemed to 'work' if it keeps patients involved with effective (for them) interventions which they would otherwise not receive. It could be deemed 'not to work' if the services it keeps patients in touch with are not effective, or if it fails to keep people in touch with effective services.

To this end it helps to understand the purpose of CCT. Here the law itself is not helpful. Compulsory treatment is simply presented as a way of compelling patients (who fulfil certain criteria) to accept services which they would otherwise refuse. The law does not say the aim is to keep people out of hospital, reduce hospital stay, prolong the time to next admission or anything else.

The criterion of significant risk (whether to self or others) implies that the CTO is in some sense to keep people (the patient and others) safe. The benefit principle indicates that the intervention must 'benefit' the person, but this can be interpreted very widely. This lack of specification of purpose could lead to different clinicians or different services interpreting the purpose of CCT differently: possibly they would not use it too differently (it has to be used within the confines of the law and the code of practice and thus is reasonably prescribed) but they might evaluate it differently.

In monitoring the use of the MHCT Act the Scottish Executive will need to have a clear understanding of what they expect from CB-CTO if they are to evaluate its usefulness, rather than simply describe for whom it has been used. Much of the research on the outcomes of CCT fails to distinguish the respective perspectives of service delivery and effectiveness of intervention.

Some evidence comes from the various community orders currently and previously available in Britain, but also from the use of such orders elsewhere, notably North America and Australasia. In many cases the outcomes used are service driven, such as re-admission to hospital or police involvement. These may have more to do with the actual services the patient receives than the CCT itself. Measuring whether the CCT has an effect involves various methodologies which could include using the person as their own 'control' or randomising patients to CCT or no CCT. It might then be necessary to control, in some way, for the interventions a person is offered, if not necessarily receiving. The methodological, ethical and legal problems with this are considerable and have been covered elsewhere (Atkinson et al, 2005). A comparison of the position in Australia, Switzerland, the UK and Canada was carried out by Dawson (2005). Two studies (described below) in the USA have managed to overcome some of these difficulties by having the law, or the courts, actively involved in the design of the study, and thus allowing for legal randomisation.

Some words of caution have to be given, however, about drawing conclusions from work in other countries. Firstly, the law itself is different. In both North America and Australia this means each state, territory or province has its own law (a position now seen more dramatically in Britain than in the past). The provisions of the CB-CTO will have to be compared with local provisions. The criteria for use of the Act in general have to be compared with local criteria. Such a comparison is by no means straightforward, as differences in the law as to powers or targeted population (e.g. whether it can be used for patients at first admission), service delivery, standards and intensity of services make for differences in outcomes which may or may not be translatable to the Scottish position.

Then there are the differences in the provision of CCT itself. In Scotland there is no difference in the criteria for compulsory treatment whether it is in the community or in hospital. There is, however, a matter of interpretation in relation to threshold of risk and consequences. If a CB-CTO is considered less 'invasive' than hospital detention, then a CB-CTO might be considered justified by a lower level of risk than a hospital-based CTO. The CB-CTO can either be granted at the initial tribunal hearing or can follow a period of inpatient treatment. This is similar to two types of orders found elsewhere.

A third type of order, the most controversial, available in some states in the USA but not in Scotland, is preventative outpatient commitment. This is used to compel treatment for people who do not reach the threshold for commitment at the time, but where there is an expectation that this will be reached if compulsory treatment is not used (Brown, 2003; Schopp, 2003). This is likely to be because it is expected that the person will, or is in the process of, stopping their treatment (usually medication).

Some who have opposed the new provisions in Scotland seem to assume that large numbers of people will be put on CB-CTOs to keep them on medication. Under the new law it is only possible to put someone on a CB-CTO, and keep them on it, if they meet all the criteria necessary for compulsory treatment. Once these criteria are no longer met the person must be discharged from the order. Thus a person who is unwell and refusing treatment, but posing no significant risk to themselves or others, cannot be compelled to have treatment. To move for an application for a CTO the significant risk criterion must be there. This creates frustration among some family members (and possibly some patients) who ask psychiatrists to intervene early in the relapse episode only to find the psychiatrists saying that they are not able to do so as the person is not ill enough. Many people want to see people treated as early as possible to prevent major exacerbation of illness and the personal and social consequences which come with this, and do not understand why this is not possible. Set against this is the need to protect people from unwanted treatment, to preserve patient choice as far as possible, and to avoid draconian intervention.

The detention of dangerous people with a severe personality disorder which has been proposed in England and Wales comes closer to this preventative commitment, although the assumption is that such people will be hospitalised.

The first randomised controlled trial of the effectiveness of CCT was carried out in North Carolina, USA on outpatient commitment orders (OPCs). This was not a study of a new legal provision as such, since OPC in North Carolina had a long history. The law was modified in 1984 to extend the criteria for its use. These include:

- having a diagnosis of a serious mental illness;
- the ability to survive in the community – given adequate support;
- a history which shows that past treatment has prevented deterioration which would lead to dangerous behaviour (defined broadly to include self and others);
- a limited ability to make informed decisions to seek or voluntarily

comply with treatment because of their mental state (Swartz et al., 2001a).

The OPC itself runs for 90 days and can be renewed for a further 180 days. The person on an OPC order is directed 'to comply' with treatment, but forcible medication of patients in the community is not permitted. Failure to comply with the order could result in the person being returned to hospital.

The research itself was sanctioned by the court, which agreed that a subgroup of involuntary patients who were waiting to be discharged could be randomised to either an OPC or a non-OPC control condition. Patients had to consent to this randomisation. A comparison group was made up of patients who were excluded from the randomisation process because of previous behaviour of serious assault, which included the use of a weapon or physical injury to another person, in the previous 12 months. Follow-up was at one year.

The study itself, however, was inevitably nothing like as tidy as this description suggests. Patients could not be held on OPC for 90 days if they could be discharged earlier. Some patients had their OPC renewed. This variation in length of time on OPC led to a criticism by Szmukler and Hotopf (2001), who suggested that the most difficult patients might be discharged from OPC because the order was 'not working', or patients who had gone missing or were in prison could be discharged, thus biasing the outcomes in favour of those most likely to be compliant with the OPC. This was countered by Swartz and Swanson (2004), who indicated that the more ill and at risk the person, the more likely they were to stay on the order. Services and service intensity were not the same for all patients, but were related to individual need and local availability.

The patients, although all meeting the criteria for commitment and compulsory treatment, were not a homogeneous group. Risk to self or risk to others was one distinction. What was called 'dual-system recidivism', meaning a history of multiple hospitalisations combined with arrest by the police and/or violence, was another important distinction, as was substance abuse.

Despite these shortcomings, this was a heroic attempt at what in any circumstances would be a difficult area to research, with complex methodology and analysis, and would almost inevitably end up with results and conclusions 'muddy' rather than clear.

The study started in 1993 and ran until 1996. The research team, headed by Marvin Swartz and Jeffrey Swanson at Duke University, made the most of what was likely to be a one-chance opportunity to carry out this work. Multiple outcomes were measured and have been reported in a series of papers. Some of the main findings have been:

Re-admission to hospital – Patients on OPC were less likely to be re-admitted to hospital than those in the control group. This was particularly true when combined with a higher intensity of outpatient services and for those who had the OPC renewed for longer than the initial 90 days. These patents also spent less time in hospital (Swartz and Swanson, 2004).

Treatment adherence – Although overall at one year follow-up no significant differences were found on treatment adherence, it was found that those who spent at least six months on OPC were more likely to adhere to medication and other treatments (Swartz et al., 2001b).

Violent behaviour – Reduced violence was associated with being on OPC for an extended period and receiving more outpatient services. Involvement with 'more than three service events' per month and staying on OPC reduced the predicted violent behaviour by half (from 48% to 24%). For those who remained on their medication and also remained substance-free the rate of violence was reduced to a predicted probability of 13% (Swanson et al., 2000; Swartz and Swanson, 2004).

Arrest by police – A range of factors are related to arrest by the police, including younger age, ethnicity, homelessness and substance use. Reduced arrest was only related to OPC for those with a history of dual-system recidivism and when the OPC was used for at least six months. The probability of arrest during the 12-month follow-up was reduced to 12% from 45% (Swanson et al., 2001).

Victim of crime – During the follow-up period, 33% of patients were victims of crime. Those on an OPC of longer duration were less likely to be a victim of crime (Hiday et al., 2002).

Perception of coercion – Patients on an OPC reported 'an increase in perceived coercion' which was related to the length of the OPC. This was, however, mediated by being reminded about the consequences of complying with the order (Swartz et al., 2003).

Quality of life – Being on an extended OPC was related to reporting a significantly higher subjective quality of life. This appeared to be related to fewer psychotic symptoms, resulting from higher adherence to treatment. This was, however, modified by the perceived coercion (Swartz et al., 2003; Swartz and Swanson; 2004).

To answer the question 'does OPC work?', Swartz and Swanson (2004) concluded that it did have positive outcomes but that it 'cannot substitute for intensity of treatment', which may be enhanced by being on an OPC (Wagner et al., 2003). OPC, they suggested, encouraged service providers to prioritise services for this group of patients and also encouraged, or motivated, patients to remain in contact with services and comply with treatment. This is a difficult conclusion to deal with in that it allows both 'sides' of the compulsory community treatment debate to claim it as a victory for their side.

The second randomised study was conducted in New York under state law, starting in 1994, when the state was considering outpatient commitment legislation (O'Reilly and Bishop, 2001; Steadman et al., 2001a, b). Seventy-eight patients received a court order. As in the North Carolina study, patients with a history of serious violent behaviour were not included in the trial. All patients received an enhanced care package, although there were considerable problems in running the study. It was conducted as a pilot, so there was no time for the service or procedures to become established, and a vital part of the procedure, namely the inclusion of the New York Police Department in 'pick-up orders for non-compliance', was not enacted. This meant that patients on an OPC order who did not comply with medication did not receive involuntary medication. Elsewhere it was suggested that services treated both groups similarly as part of the 'Bellevue programme' (Swartz and Swanson, 2004).

With some patients unavailable for follow-up at 11 months, small numbers made for problems in analysis and interpretation (Steadman et al., 2001a, b). In comparing the group who were on an OPC order with those who were not, some of the findings were:

Hospitalisation – No significant differences were found between the groups, except that those on OPC had significantly fewer multiple hospitalisations.

Days in hospital – Although there was no significant difference between the groups, the median for the OPC group was 43 days compared with 101 for the control group. This difference might be practically significant to both patients and services.

Number of arrests – No significant difference.

Quality of life – No significant difference.

Symptomatology – No significant difference.

Although these two studies look as though they come to different conclusions, the methodological problems, particularly in New York, mean that the outcomes should be treated with some caution and we should look to combine these findings with other studies. Without the sanction of the law or courts, randomised trials are not possible. Other studies have attempted, with difficulty, to use matched control designs (Preston et al., 2002) or retrospective case control studies (e.g. several unpublished postgraduate theses cited by Dawson, 2005). These, plus a number of authors (Gerbasi et al., 2000; Hiday, 2003; Swartz and Swanson, 2004; Dawson, 2005; Erickson, 2005; Lawton-Smith, 2005) have suggested that there are positive benefits to patients from CCT. These include, in general, therapeutic benefits; greater compliance with treatment regimes, including medication; reduced hospital admissions; improved quality of life, including family relationships;

and reduced involvement in violence and self-harm. A Cochrane review, however, suggested that CCT makes no significant difference on a variety of measures, including service use, social functioning or quality of life, when compared with standard care (Kisley et al., 2005). A review by the RAND Institute was equivocal and pointed to the need, among other evaluations, for a good economic evaluation (Ridgley et al., 2001).

To really understand how useful CCT may be there is a need to understand the population which is subject to it. In all the studies mentioned demographic data is either reported differently or missing. The most that can be said is that CCT is used predominately with single men with a psychotic disorder, usually schizophrenia, and a substantial number have concurrent substance abuse. Although different ethnic groups are sometimes reported this was usually not given with population numbers with which to compare rates.

As noted earlier, views about CB-CTO were varied during the discussions on the bill, and research where CCT is used gives a similar picture. In general patients preferred CCT where the alternative was hospitalisation (Atkinson et al., 2005; Swartz et al., 2003; Gibbs et al., 2005). Other positive aspects were the sense that services had to stay in contact with them, and their improved mental health. Set against this was the dislike of coercion, particularly in respect of medication, and other restrictions on freedom. Psychiatrists' views on CCT vary to some extent with the powers they have, but experience of using CCT tended to increase positive views (Atkinson et al., 1997, 2000; Dawson, 2005). Additional paperwork was disliked. In general there was a view that the positive benefits outweighed the coercion involved (Dawson and Romans, 2001).

To understand the use of the new CB-CTO in Scotland, individual data need to be routinely collected, including demographic data; ICD-10 diagnosis; services and treatment received, including hospitalisation and for how long; agreed clinical outcomes; frequency of use of services; and relationship with other services such as social work, voluntary organisations and the criminal justice system. This would give a good indication of how useful CB-CTOs may be across the country, and should then be supplemented with qualitative studies describing views and experiences. This will be important in order to understand CB-CTOs in respect of the principle of least restrictive alternative, which underpinned their introduction.

Note

1. In Britain capacity is the legal term and competence is usually used as the clinical term. In the USA competence is sometimes the legal term. In many cases they are used interchangeably, although care should be taken to be clear whether a legal judgement has been made.

Chapter 3

The Mental Health Tribunal for Scotland

The process by which patients were subject to long-term detention and compulsory treatment under the 1984 Act was through the sheriff court, which also heard appeals. This caused some concern as comparatively few patients, their nearest relative or their representatives appeared in court (Bean et al., 2000). Thus it was not clear that their views were being heard or their rights upheld. In many cases the main medical witness did not appear in court and the case was decided on the basis of written evidence. Evidence given to the Parliamentary Committee reviewing the bill suggested that the role of the sheriff court was not always well understood and there was stigma attached to going to court:

> appearing in front of the sheriff. I did not have a parking ticket or speeding fine, but the procedure I had to go through to be put under section was degrading. I went to the sheriff court once, but on other occasions when section 18s were put on me I felt so bad that I did not even go to court. We are people. Yes, we have an illness but no, we are not criminals. Why treat us in such a way? (Maggie Keppie, Edinburgh Users Forum, in Scottish Parliament, 2002f, col. 3287)

> I had never been to court before and found it to be quite a terrifying experience. My mind was going round in circles as to what was going to happen next. (Marcia Reid, Highland Users Group, in Scottish Parliament, 2002f, col. 3272)

The Millan Committee looked at the mental health tribunal system, particularly as it applied in England and Wales, and was persuaded that this would be a better option. In England and Wales however, the Mental Health Review Tribunal (MHRT) does not admit people but only hears appeals against detention (under the 1983 Act). This is not to say that the system in England and Wales is without problems (Atkinson et al., 2005). Of particular concern have been the cost of running the increasing number of tribunals (Department of Health, 2002b); delays in arranging them (Hewitt, 1999); and general problems in running them, from delays in receiving paperwork to staffing issues (Crossley, 2004).

The Millan Committee suggested that a mental health tribunal system be introduced to replace the sheriff court in relation to mental health legislation. There was widespread support for an independent tribunal system:

> In general we are in favour of tribunals, although some people say that the seriousness of what we go through merits the formality of the justice system and the justice that it offers. Most of us say that we want an informal system; one that is fair and in which people's opinions are heard and in which they are not frightened. (Graham Morgan, Highland Users Group, in Scottish Parliament, 2002f, col. 3271)

The Law Society of Scotland supported tribunals, although some may have preferred a specialised, designated sheriff (Scottish Parliament, 2002f). However:

> The Law Society's mental health and disability committee may have different views on that ... some of us greatly prefer tribunals, because of their greater informality and the input from people other than lawyers ... some of us are excited about and welcome the prospect of mental health tribunals. (Hilary Patrick, Law Society of Scotland, in Scottish Parliament, 2002f, col. 3248)

It was seen as a destigmatising move; one that would make it more likely that patients would be able to attend and take part in the proceedings. Unlike the current system in England and Wales, the new Mental Health Tribunal for Scotland (MHTS) would have the power to detain, as well as discharge, patients. The only group to clearly oppose the move to tribunals were the sheriffs themselves. They suggested the need to separate the questions of compulsion and treatment, and that:

> If you consider that the issues of the liberty of the subject are as important as we believe them to be, you can say that the Executive has got it wrong and that the Parliament should not give its approval to the setting up of the tribunal. (Sheriff Richard Scott, Sheriffs' Association, in Scottish Parliament, 2002g, col. 3321)

Other issues raised by the Sheriffs' Association were the independence of the sheriff court; that people are used to dealing with evidence; that in the sheriff courts there are no local pressures and no concerns about hospital funding; and that with 49 sheriff courts they are easily available. In a roundabout way tribunals were described as:

> An inexpert body that does not have experience of assessing evidence, or of being dispassionate and keeping its prejudices out of decisions ... The court affords total impartiality and careful consideration of the issues ... We examine whether, on the basis of the material that is before us, the law has been satisfied ... We have

> the advantage of coming to cases with a completely open mind and with expertise in decision making. (Sheriff Richard Scott, Sheriffs' Association, in Scottish Parliament, 2002g, col. 3326)

The point was made that it is not the attending of the sheriff court that intimidates people, but the prospect of having their liberty taken away. This is something which research on people's experiences with tribunals may answer.

A concern was raised in relation to the similar proposals in England and Wales, where it was suggested that taking a legal approach in the tribunal, including legal language and style of debate, might harm both therapeutic relationships and clinical decision-making (Obomanu and Kennedy, 2001). It was perceived as a problem that the medical member carrying out a preliminary examination of the patient was being both 'witness and decision-maker' (Richardson and Machin, 2000). Perhaps surprisingly, Millan proposed the same system in Scotland, but this received criticism from a number of sources and was not included in the bill.

Although the move to tribunals was welcomed, some concern was expressed as to the extent of the additional work required and the implications of this for the workforce, particularly psychiatrists (Atkinson et al., 2002d) and MHOs (McCollam et al., 2003). This issue is discussed in the final chapter.

McManus and Thomson (2005) noted that, while 'instinctively it appears desirable to move such proceedings out of court and to a more informal setting', reflection on the practice in England and Wales indicated that 'these tribunals have often been prolonged and extremely adversarial'. It would seem that promoting the principle of participation would involve more than just setting up tribunals. There was an assumption that having access to an independent advocate might make patients more likely to attend tribunal hearings, as would having them in more informal places.

As in other areas of mental health law there is comparatively little research on experience with tribunals.

The experience of tribunals

Although there was an expectation from Millan and others that tribunals would encourage participation by patients, this has not always been apparent in practice. A study of MHRTs by Ferencz and McGuire (2000) concluded that the tribunal process was viewed very differently by patients and tribunal members. Tribunal members thought the tribunal was fairer and more independent than did patients. It also seemed that patients' knowledge about the tribunal was limited and they needed to know more about both its roles and how it operates.

It might be expected, or at least hoped, that patients in a high security hospital would have good knowledge of the tribunal process. However, a study of patients in Ashworth Hospital in 1995 suggested otherwise (Dolan et al., 1999). Of 70 patients only 9% had any accurate knowledge of the powers of tribunals, and all but six patients believed the tribunal had powers that it did not have. It seemed that neither the clinical nor the legal team was explaining the procedures fully, with the suggestion that the clinical team saw this as the lawyer's role. While this might be expected to have implications for patients being able to exert their rights, there was in fact no relationship between knowledge and the number of applications made. There was some suggestion that patients used the procedures as a way of measuring their progress. This, coupled with another study indicating that in the special hospitals 90% of tribunals made no change to the patient's status, would suggest that tribunals in special hospitals are an expensive exercise which may not be the best use of resources in securing patients' rights (Taylor et al., 1999).

An informal survey of MHOs suggested that in Scotland patients were more likely to attend the tribunal or be represented by an advocate than previously, although in some cases representation was less, particularly for people with dementia and learning disability (Mental Health Officer Newsletter, in press).

The Mental Health Tribunal for Scotland

The Mental Health Tribunal for Scotland was established by the MHCT Act (Pt 3, s. 21 and Sch. 2) and is sponsored by the Scottish Executive. It is made up of two distinct parts. There is the Tribunal itself,[1] which is a non-departmental public body, and an Administration. Establishing the MHTS marked 'a fundamental change in the way decisions are made about the long-term compulsory care and treatment of people in Scotland who suffer from a mental disorder' (Scottish Executive, 2005e).

The Tribunal has at its head a full-time, publicly appointed President. The first President is Mrs Eileen Davie. Having started her career as a psychiatric social worker, she was latterly an advocate with extensive experience of the tribunal system in children's panels. There are approximately 300 tribunal panel members: these are part-time public appointments. It is the panel members who are responsible for the judicial functioning of the tribunal hearings and who make the decisions about patients' compulsory care and treatment. The panel members fall into three categories: legal, medical and general members (Mental Health Tribunal for Scotland, 2004a, b, c). To be eligible, the legal member has to be a solicitor or advocate of at least seven years' standing; the medical member has to be 'experienced in the diagnosis and treatment of mental disorders', and general members must have experience or qualifications in social care facilities. This is broadly interpreted to include being a user of mental health services or a carer. At the end of September 2005 there were 137 general members, including service users, carers, nurses, clinical psychologists, social workers, occupational therapists and people employed in or managing the provision of a care service. The two largest groups were social workers and nurses, who made up 70% of the total (www.mhtscot.org).

Members are normally appointed for five years. There is provision for this to be renewed – the criteria include satisfactory performance. Members are expected to be involved in hearings for at least two days each month. To maintain the independence of the hearings, members 'should have no professional connection which could conflict with matters falling within the tribunal's jurisdiction'. All members have to undergo training before being able to take part in hearings. Tribunal members are paid, with the legal member – who arguably has more work – being paid most. The medical and general members are paid the same.

The Administration is responsible for the day-to day running of the Tribunal, including case-management, scheduling tribunal hearings, matters to do with finance and communications, and providing local support to tribunal hearings. Its staff, approximately 45 of them, are Scottish Executive civil servants. They are based mainly at the Tribunal's headquarters in Hamilton, South Lanarkshire, in line with the Scottish Executive's policy to disperse jobs throughout Scotland.

The aim of the MHTS is, according to its website 'to provide a responsive, accessible, independent and impartial service when making decisions on the compulsory care and treatment of people with mental health problems'. This is underpinned by 'the core values of professionalism, independence, and inclusiveness', as shown in six areas of functioning:

- handling cases sensitively and responsively;
- taking full account of the needs and rights of individuals;
- engaging proactively with stakeholders;
- ensuring hearings' environments are fair and impartial;
- providing clear and timely information on our processes;
- maximising efficient and effective use of public resources. (www.mhtscot.org)

Although the main work of the tribunals is expected to be to hear applications for a CTO, they will also deal with appeals against short-term detention and CTOs, interim extension orders, variations to orders, the mandatory reviews of orders, referrals coming from Scottish Ministers or the Mental Welfare Commission, and restricted patient orders.

The first task of the Tribunal was to establish procedures. A consultation exercise was carried out over the winter of 2004-5 on the draft of practice and procedure rules (Scottish Parliament, 2004). A number of areas proved particularly contentious, not least whether the hearings were to be in public or private, and also the location of hearings. The rules also needed revisiting as they did not always match the Act. The final document was laid before the Scottish Parliament on 29 August 2005 (Scottish Parliament, 2005)

Tribunal members

The relationship between the three members of a tribunal will be crucial to both the way the tribunal functions and the decisions it reaches. The tribunal is a legal entity working with legal criteria within what is seen as a clinical context. This, it is suggested, can cause tension between the paternalism which underlies much of the mental health legislation and the common law's emphasis on personal freedom (Wood, 1999).

The tribunal will be convened by the legal member except where the patient is subject to a compulsion order, hospital order or a transfer for treatment direction. In such cases the convenor will be either a sheriff or the Tribunal President.

Not everyone is happy with the make-up of the tribunal panel, and the fight for dominance between law and medicine has already begun. A polemical article largely against the power of psychiatrists was published in the Journal of the Law Society of Scotland a month after the tribunals came into being. In it, Turner (2005) used anecdote to suggest that in England (some) medical members dominate proceedings, that many of his clients distrust psychiatrists, and that nurses should not be general members as they are the 'same profession' as medicine and subservient to medical practitioners. There is little evidence to support or refute such claims.

Psychiatrists themselves had raised concerns about the amount of time which will be taken out of their normal clinical practice by having to sit on tribunals. One way to manage this is for retiring and recently retired psychiatrists to serve on tribunals. Concerns that such people may be becoming out of date should be offset by the current requirements for CPD (continuing professional development) and appraisal in the NHS. These requirements are also likely to limit the time for which a retired psychiatrist would continue to be accredited.

In England and Wales the question has arisen of whether being the medical member of the MHRT gives the doctor an unrealistic dual role. It is suggested that for the medical member to carry out a preliminary medical examination may prejudice their thinking (Prins, 2000; Richardson and Machin, 2000), although this has been challenged (Gibson, 2000).

Turner's (2005) point that 'I had observed over the years that many of my clients who had experience of compulsory medication and detention had a deep mistrust of their psychiatrists', while possibly true, is not necessarily the only view of psychiatrists. It is likely that those people who refuse treatment, and possibly also deny illness or problems, are more likely to mistrust those who propose such treatment. This mistrust might be rational or based on distorted thinking due to illness. Not everyone has trust in the legal profession, but this does not lead to a suggestion there should not be sheriffs or judges.

Much will depend on the way in which the tribunal conducts its business. All members have received the same training and all have a duty to bear in mind the principles underlying the Act when making their decisions. This should help to shape common ground as well as bring different perspectives to the tribunal. These, Ross (2005) suggests, will allow the tribunal to 'set and maintain' the 'inclusive and informal tone' which is laid out as appropriate in the rules for the tribunals.

There is some limited evidence on decision-making in tribunals in England (Peay, 1989), although the dual nature of the medical role makes it difficult to extrapolate from this to the new Scottish situation. Peay (2003, 2005) has also explored difficulties between psychiatrists and approved social workers in decision-making in relation to the detention process.

The tribunal process has been studied more recently in the Mental Health Review Board (MHRB) system in Victoria, Australia which also has a legal chair, a psychiatrist and a community member (who represents the views of the community). Swain (2000) analysed 25 hearings during 1997-8. The most active member was the legal member, in all issues raised during the hearing, including in relation to treatment. Overall the community member was least active, asking fewer questions. Even though the community member was most active in exploring the patient's case and making sure the patient understood what was going on, this was still less than the legal member. Jaworowski and Guneva (2002) found no significant difference in the consistency of decision-making between clinicians and MHRB members.

Responding to a questionnaire, community members indicated that they felt marginalised and that they were less 'useful' than the professional members were. Both legal and medical members attested to the importance of the community members' role, even though it seemed to be less defined than the others. In particular, the community member was seen as important in understanding the patient and their behaviour, beliefs and situation from a non-professional perspective, and also useful in dealing with some of the patients' reactions. Their role was:

> Perceived by their colleagues as important to the achievement of statutory procedural fairness for the whole range of tribunal constituents, rather than just those who are astute, articulate or sufficiently well prepared to make good use of the hearing process. (Swain, 2000)

Also, the community member was seen by other members as being more of an 'individual'; it was their personal skills and experience which were valued rather than those coming from formal training in a particular discipline.

Tribunal hearings

An interesting conundrum raised over tribunal hearings illustrates that people's various rights do not always lie well together. Under human rights legislation, court proceedings (in most circumstances) have to take place in public. Justice not only has to be done but also has to be seen to be done. This is undoubtedly a way of protecting the rights of those subject to court proceedings. At the same time people are entitled to privacy. Previously, most section 18 applications had been heard informally in chambers (at the sheriff court), with a few heard in hospitals (Bean et al., 2000).

There was an expectation in some quarters early on that the tribunal would be held in public. That was certainly the expectation of the Scottish Executive, and of the Council on Tribunals. Interestingly, it was not the expectation of the Sheriffs' Association and contributed to its objection to tribunals (Scottish Parliament, 2002g). Eileen Davie, the incoming President, also believed that to comply with the European Convention on Human Rights tribunals had to be held in public. There was also some, possibly naïve, hope that this might help to dispel some of the stigma attached to having a mental illness or being subject to the Act. Few other people agreed.

In particular, patient/user groups, carer groups and the Royal College of Psychiatrists (Scottish Division) were adamantly opposed to public hearings. They had what might be a more cynical, but ultimately more realistic view on stigma, which was that public tribunal hearings would only add to it. Given the detail that could be presented about a patient's medical history, past and present social and personal circumstances, and current medical position, it is understandable that anyone would want the right to privacy, even if a mental illness were not involved. It was clear that if hearings were held in public many people would never attend, or never appeal, and any safeguards or advantages in the new system would be lost. The privacy argument won the day, Eileen Davie changed her mind and hearings will now normally be held in private.

Another issue had been where the tribunals were to be held. A number of user groups were hoping the tribunals would be held in community locations, away from hospitals or NHS premises. This, they believed, would help ensure the independence of the tribunal. The tribunal would certainly look more independent but it is debatable whether it would make any real difference to the process. The Scottish Executive seemed to assume that tribunals would be held in NHS premises and that there were plenty of appropriate rooms available. It is conceivable that not a few hospitals took pleasure in pointing out that since so much hospital property had been sold off there was not necessarily the space easily available to set up a tribunal hearing system.

Pragmatism won, and it is expected that the majority of tribunals will be heard in the hospital in which the patient is currently an in-patient (Scottish Executive, 2005a). There is some indication, however, that in some places (such as Glasgow) where there is more than one hospital tribunals will only be held in certain designated locations and patients will have to travel if they want to attend. The code of practice suggests that where the person is not an in-patient a venue 'as near as possible to where that person resides' should be used (Scottish Executive, 2005a).

Legal and clinical considerations at hearings

First and foremost the tribunal is a judicial process making a legal decision to take away someone's freedom (or aspects of that freedom). Tribunal members are there to deliver a statute. That the clinical might take over from the judicial has been highlighted by the Scottish Committee of the Council on Tribunals (2005):

> Our overriding fear is that this tribunal is being seen as a further case discussion on patients' treatment and hospitalisation rather than part of the administrative justice system. This does not bode well. (p. 9)
>
> Six months into the new system there was some suggestion that the tribunal does facilitate a discussion of the patient's welfare and puts the patient 'at the centre of the process'. (Mental Health Officer Newsletter, in press)

Although some changes to an order may be possible at the tribunal they may be less than some people suppose. Since the care plan has to be prepared this will be for either a hospital-based or community-based order. Changing the application from one to the other will not be possible, or at least very difficult, at the hearing, as there will be no appropriate plan in place. Another hearing would then be needed, but this raises the question of what to do in the interim. This means that the care plan needs to be revisited in the last few days to take account of any changes in the patient's circumstances. The timetable is thus fairly tight and the workload considerable.

The large number of people who could want to give evidence at a tribunal may make the proceedings very long, lasting a number of hours. A patient who is unwell is unlikely to be able to concentrate for that length of time and thus, even if present, may not really be aware of all that is going on.

The tribunals themselves will be tape recorded: it is considered to be in the patient's interest to have a full record of the evidence given if there is an appeal. This was opposed by some at first, out of concern for some patients' possible paranoia. There is therefore the opportunity to take notes if this is more appropriate.

It is clear that a close watch will be kept on the process of the tribunals for some time, to manage 'glitches' in the system and to aim for consistency of practice.

Note

1. There is a convention in much of the writing to use Tribunal when referring to the parent body, the MHTS, and tribunal when referring to individual tribunal hearings. This convention will be followed in this chapter.

Chapter 4

Patients' Rights and Safeguards

The MHCT Act has made a considered effort to balance the rights of patients and the protection of the public where there might be risk. Safeguarding patients and their rights can come from two different approaches. One is a 'best interest' stance, which means it is appropriate to treat people who are unable to take decisions for themselves. The assumption is that people would rather be well than ill, live rather than die. In mental health this means that people can be treated under statutory powers.

The second approach is one of civil liberties and seeks to promote the patient's autonomy and choice, even if this means they remain unwell. The enthusiastic promotion of this approach in the USA, coupled with the decline in hospital beds, led to the telling phrase 'dying with their right on' to describe people who refused treatment but were too ill to function in society. It applies particularly to people whose risk is to themselves rather than to others. The principle of participation is also important here. Patients who are able to participate in decisions about their treatment and care will necessarily be expressing more autonomy.

There are many examples of enhancing patients rights throughout the MHCT Act. Not least is the provision of a set of principles and the charge to the Mental Welfare Commission to uphold these. There are specific safeguards for some treatments such as ECT and neurosurgery for mental disorder. The enhanced position of carers, including the appointment of a named person (see next chapter), may work to support patients' rights. There is also the right to an independent advocacy service. Possibly the most innovative is the introduction of advance statements, which this chapter will consider in some detail: since it allows patients to refuse treatment, this new right requires some brief consideration. Underpinning all these safeguards, however, is the introduction of the impaired decision-making criterion.

Advocacy

The MHCT Act gives people the right of access to an independent advocate and puts a duty on both local authorities and the NHS to provide this service (s. 259). Along with this are additional rights to provision of information (s. 260) and assistance to patients who have communication difficulties (s. 261).

The right to advocacy was an important issue for most of the service users and their representatives who responded during the whole consultation process (Scottish Parliament, 2002e, f)

An advocate is described as someone who: 'enables the patient to "find their voice" and to express their views' (Scottish Executive, 2005f). Its centrality to a user perspective of services had been demonstrated earlier in the Scottish Executive's *Independent Advocacy: A Guide for Commissioners* (2000), which set out the principles for independent advocacy. The Act defines advocacy as:

> Services or support and representation made available for the purpose of enabling the person to whom they are available to have as much control of, or capacity to influence, that person's care and welfare as is, in the circumstances, appropriate. (s. 259(4))

The code of practice sets this out as being 'to help a patient to understand their options and convey their views' (Scottish Executive, 2005a). The code also makes it clear that having an advocate involved does not alter the responsibilities of other professionals towards the patient. The Act also makes specific provision for individual advocacy services at the State Hospital – a service that has been in existence for some time (Atkinson and McPherson, 2001).

Two bodies currently exist in Scotland to promote and develop advocacy services across the board: the Advocacy Standards Agency and the Scottish Independent Advocacy Alliance. There is, however, general acknowledgement that services will have to expand. There are various models of advocacy, which can be summarised as individual advocacy, collective advocacy and citizen advocacy. The expectation is that the focus will be on providing individual advocacy. This will be for all people with mental health problems. In relation to people subject to the Act, it is likely that advocates will have a role in supporting patients at a tribunal hearing. The hope has been expressed that this will increase patients' participation in the proceedings. It may also be important in enabling people to make an advance statement.

A guide to advocacy for service users sets out what might be provided and distinguishes between professional and citizen advocacy (Scottish Executive, 2005f).

What impact an increased use of advocacy will have on patients' involvement with services is unclear, as is any impact on how it will help patients in relation to the legal process. A scoping exercise by the Royal College of Psychiatrists' Scottish Division considering the possible implications of the new legislation on workforce issues adopted a neutral position on the impact of advocacy (Atkinson et al., 2002d). This reflected the view that enabling the patient's voice to be heard may lengthen proceedings in some circumstances, but contribute to a speedier outcome in others.

Refusal of treatment

Implicit in the provision to make advance statements is the opportunity for some people to refuse treatment and to expect this choice to be honoured. The implications of this are not altogether clear, for individuals or services, and in the latter case will certainly depend on the number of people involved. There will be implications for demand on beds (where a person is nevertheless detained but remains untreated): even a small number of patients could place an excessive strain on the service (Szmukler and Holloway, 1998). Some patients may remain ill for some considerable time, requiring long-term beds, which have largely been closed under previous policy decisions.

Some states in the USA have provision for refusal of treatment, but the number of people who refuse all treatment is currently small. Some legislation has put a limit on the length of time for which a person can refuse medication. In Vermont, Act 114 1998 essentially allowed a patient 45 days of not being treated before the hospital could petition the court to overturn this for someone who was incompetent and involuntarily committed. This could be seen as a compromise in giving the patient time to start improving from their acute relapse before instigating treatment, without the hospital having to keep an untreated, severely ill patient for too long. This position was challenged by Nancy Hargrave (Appelbaum, 2004). The intention was to stop the state (through the hospital) ever being able to override her advance directive refusing medication. The challenge, based on the Americans with Disabilities Act 1990, was upheld by the court. Appelbaum saw this decision as likely to cause problems for the future if advance directives now mean that, apart from emergency treatment, a person could not be treated 'even when the alternative is long term institutional care', with the consequence that hospitals will fill with patients who can neither be treated nor, because of commitment orders, discharged.

There is also the question of how people who refuse medication are to be managed while ill. If they pose no risk, the law allows them to continue to live in the community, remaining ill or deteriorating until they can be treated under the Act. If the patient is in hospital, risk behaviour has to be managed. Risk to other patients may not just be through overt aggression and violence, but may also contribute to a less-than-therapeutic atmosphere on the ward. Risk of violence, which may be to both staff and other patients, will have to be managed by non-medication means. This could include restraint and seclusion. Even where a patient chooses restraint or seclusion over medication its use has an impact on the whole service. It is witnessed by patients, to whom it may never apply, but who will nevertheless suffer trauma and distress (Frueh et al., 2005; Robbins et al., 2005).

There is little research on the use of restraint in Britain particularly outside nursing homes or forensic situations. The inquiry following the death of David 'Rocky' Bennett in 1998 while being restrained highlighted a number of concerns (Blofeld, 2003). There are guidelines for the use of restraint (Royal College of Psychiatrists Research Unit 1998, Mental Welfare Commission for Scotland 1998, NICE 2005).

Care must be taken not to assume that violent or assaultive behaviour is necessarily a result of treatment refusal, or that treatment refusal leads to assaultive behaviour.

The use of control and restraint techniques in the NHS has followed from procedures first used in the prison service and then high security special hospitals (Lee et al., 2001). Training programmes have developed in both the UK and the USA (Infantino and Musingo, 1985; Collins, 1994; Phillips and Rudestam, 1995; Beech, 1999; Lee et al., 2001).

In the USA, where the right to refuse treatment has been upheld in many states, seclusion and restraint are more common and used more routinely than in Britain (Atkinson et al., 2005), and it has become a priority to reduce their use (Curie, 2005; Glover, 2005). Programmes to reduce their routine use have involved increased use of medication, including with patients who had previously refused medication and behavioural programmes. The specifics of these depend on the individual, the nature of the behaviour, and service resources, including staff training (Fisher, 2003; Donat, 2005; Smith et al., 2005).

All behaviour has consequences and not all are anticipated. Being able to refuse treatment is a promotion of patient choice. It is not, however, a neutral decision. Many patients who refuse treatment such as medication will not be left alone, as they may hope, but will still be detained in hospital and subject to other forms of 'management' or treatment they would also prefer to avoid. Patients may choose what is the least restrictive alternative for them through an advance statement (Atkinson and Garner, 2002). Everyone – patients, staff, politicians and the public – has to recognise that in some instances there are no optimal choices, only 'least bad' ones.

> Using force with another human being is not a pleasant experience and is to be avoided at all costs ... it diminishes the people who are using violence as well. (Dr Denise Coia, Royal College of Psychiatrists, in Scottish Parliament, 2002e, col. 3226).

Commitment to appropriate, humane management of disturbed and/or violent behaviour is necessary, preserving patients' dignity as far as possible. But not everyone has the same hierarchy of choices. This brief consideration of restraint and seclusion is not intended to imply that their use will increase under the MHCT Act. It is simply a reminder that the right to refuse treatment may bring with it some unintended or unexpected consequences which have not generally been explored with people. Neither are they the only response to medication refusal. Behavioural and psychological programmes also have their place.

Advance statements

Advance statements allow people to plan, when competent in the present, for treatment decisions in the future when they are unable to make them. They are an innovation in the MHCT Act. They have been greeted with some enthusiasm and considerable expectation by users in some quarters. For others this has been tempered by the concern that they can be overturned, or about other issues.

> Most members of HUG [Highland Users Group] think that advance statements are the solution, although some members think there could be problems ... I am worried that people will get stuck in limbo ... I worry that a past view ... might put a person into stasis if the statement cannot be changed ... Common sense should be used, although a great deal of emphasis should be put on advance statements as an effective method of presenting views ... I guess that most people would say that advance statements should be listened to, but that there should be circumstances in which they may be overturned. Some HUG members would say that advance statements should be binding ... even though they later seem to be illogical ... our members have conflicting opinions on this matter. (Graham Morgan, Highland Users Group, in Scottish Parliament, 2002f, cols 3268–9)

They are not legally binding: the treating psychiatrist does not have to follow the statement implicitly and without regard to consequences, but it is expected that, in the general rule of things, they will be followed. If, for whatever reason, a psychiatrist does not want to follow, or is unable to comply with, an advance statement, they have to explain why, in writing, to the patient, their named person, their welfare attorney, their guardian and the Mental Welfare Commission, and also put a copy into the person's medical record. When the care plan is approved at the tribunal, any advance statement will be taken into consideration.

Before looking at the issues involved in making an advance statement it is worth putting their arrival in Scotland in some historical and policy context and then looking at their use elsewhere, notably the USA. There are a variety of terms in the literature, the most common being 'advance directives' (Atkinson et al., 2003a). All allow for decision-making for the future. For ease, 'advance directive' will be used here as the generic term and 'advance statement' will be used only in reference to the MHCT Act.

The context of advance statements in Scotland

Advance directives are available throughout Britain under common law. They are usually seen as referring to advance refusal of treatment (British

Medical Association, 1995) and, because of their association with end-of-life situations, are often referred to as living wills.

In the USA, however, the notion of advance directives in mental health has been around since the 1980s (Atkinson et al., 2003a, Atkinson, in press). These advance directives can include both refusal (opt-out) of treatment and acceptance of treatment (opt-in).

During the 1990s interest was expressed in the potential usefulness of advance directives in many situations in mental health, but how this would be implemented and what 'advance directive' actually meant were rarely spelt out (Atkinson and Patterson, 2000). There were two approaches. One approach, promoting and respecting patient choice and self-advocacy, frequently came from a civil liberties perspective. The other approach was that of developing and improving the relationship and communication between patient and doctor. In such cases the documents were more likely to be described as advance agreements or joint crisis plans (Atkinson et al., 2003a; Atkinson, in press).

User groups and voluntary organisations were also showing an interest in forms of advance directive. MDF The BiPolar Organisation, for example, has supported the use of advance directives or crisis cards for some time, and have produced guides to writing these. The internet has proved a fruitful source of information on writing advance directives in mental health for users, with many states in the USA providing examples to fit their own laws.

The main themes to emerge from a study investigating stakeholders' views in Scotland were their legal status; whether they were opt-in or opt-out, made independently of staff or co-operatively with them; the range of care or decisions covered; and the provision (or not) for the appointment of proxies (Atkinson et al., 2003b). These were distilled into four main models (with two variations) that might be expected within the parameters of British law.

Described in general terms they were:

1. patient-initiated; could be overruled by mental health law;
2. co-operatively made between patient and doctor; could be overruled by mental health law;
3. independent or co-operative; opt out of treatment; legally binding (i.e. cannot be overruled by mental health law);
4. independent or co-operative; opt in to treatment (i.e. acceptance of treatment when ill and refusing); may or may not involve a proxy.

Two variations were suggested for models 3 and 4, and were restricted to decisions about ECT since this was the area which had engendered most passion, and controversy, in the interviews and groups (Atkinson et al., 2003b).

These models were presented to various groups of stakeholders throughout Britain in a postal questionnaire to gauge views (Atkinson et al., 2004b).

There were 450 responses. There was general support to the question 'do you think we need advance directives?' from voluntary organisations (89%), directors of social work/social service (82%), CPNs (79%), directors of mental health trusts (71%) and MHOs (66%). Sadly, and possibly worryingly for the implementation of advance statements, only 28% of psychiatrists responded positively to this question. In response to the opt-in and opt-out models (3 and 4 above), psychiatrists were significantly less likely to want to work with the opt-out models than other groups. Interestingly, in no group was there a majority in favour of model 4, the opt-in model where patients agree in advance to particular treatments. This might seem surprising at first sight – it might be expected that psychiatrists, at least, would welcome patients opting into treatment – but there are many clinical and legal issues which make this procedure less than straightforward (Atkinson, in press).

Advance statements in the Mental Health (Care and Treatment) (Scotland) Act 2003

Advance statements are introduced in sections 275 and 276 of the new Act. The notable features of the Scottish legislation are that it allows for:

- patients to make both opt-in and opt-out decisions;
- advance statements to be followed even though someone is subject to the Act;
- a clear process for making them, witnessing them, consulting them and implementing them.

The advance statement applies only to treatment decisions. As previously noted, however, treatment is widely interpreted in the Act. Nevertheless, it is unlikely to cover as much as some people would want. To enable people to make their wider views known, the provision has been introduced to make a personal statement (Scottish Executive, 2004b). This does not have the same legal standing as the advance statement but is intended to cover the range of areas about which people are likely to have concerns or need to make decisions. Obvious examples are choices regarding care of children and provision for childcare (which would have to comply with the Children Act 1989) or care of pets. The Scottish Executive also suggested that the personal statement may cover aspects of life such as how the person likes 'to exercise or relax'. The personal statement will give a much broader picture of the person, their wishes and life choices, and may help to put some of their treatment decisions in context. Reasons for decisions can be included in the personal statement or in the advance directive itself. An example is given of helpful, additional information: 'I don't want medication which might make me put on weight' (Scottish Executive, 2004b).

Although anyone can make an advance statement it is anticipated that they will be made by people who have a recurring mental illness which impairs their capacity to make decisions about their care and treatment, especially if this means they are likely to become subject to the MHCT Act. This is, therefore, most likely to be people with a diagnosis of schizophrenia, bi-polar disorder, other psychosis or severe depression. There is, however, nothing to stop anyone making an advance statement, and people who may be at risk of developing such disorders (for example through family history) may want to make one. The guide to advance statements published by the Scottish Executive (2004b), which outlines how to make one in line with the new law, describes it as being 'primarily for people who use mental health services'.

There are many practical issues in making and using an advance statement. One way of considering these is to look at each stage of the process and the general decisions to be made.

Making an advance statement

Making an advance statement involves, in theory, all the same issues and requirements as making a contemporaneous decision, and so the same regard needs to be given to informed consent. The only difference is that the decision will be implemented in the future, which arguably requires some additional consideration.

Clearly the most important requirement is that the person is capable of making the decision. Two aspects may be important. Does the person have the capacity to understand what an advance statement is? And do they have the capacity to make a medical decision? In the light of the criteria for compulsory treatment it is the latter which may be the more important. A tool designed specifically to assess competence to make an advance directive has been developed in the USA (Srebnik et al., 2004). It is not clear how the people who witness an advance statement are expected to assess capacity, and it is unlikely that they will all approach this from a clinical perspective.

An additional consideration in making an advance statement is how much things may change between making the advance statement and the time it is implemented. The easiest way to deal with this is to have the advance statement reviewed frequently so that the decision can either be updated in line with new developments in treatment or confirmed. A possible limitation to frequent updates is that the advance statement will have to be witnessed each time. How easy this would be to organise and repeat at intervals remains to be seen. Pressure on staff time may mean this is not seen as a priority. Any costs – to pay a solicitor, for example –could be covered by legal aid. It is not intended that costs should accrue to the individual which might make an advance statement unaffordable for them. In the USA, however, where the organisation of health care is funded through insurance, the question has arisen as to whether time spent writing an advance directive with a patient, advising on it, or related activities is 'billable', or chargeable, to the patient or their insurance company (Srebnik and Brodoff, 2003).

Another approach is to write an advance statement in more general terms that make the underlying reasons clear but give some leeway as to interpretation. For instance, the previous example of not wanting medication which leads to weight gain would allow for a range of other medication based on the doctor's clinical opinion. This may be a 'safer' (i.e. less likely to be overruled) approach than writing 'I will only take y', unless there is very good reason why this is the only appropriate medication. Even with an advance statement a doctor cannot be compelled to prescribe medication or give other treatment against their clinical judgement.

A further consideration which might be useful to include in any advance statement is evidence that the person has given due consideration to the consequences. The most likely parameters here are time span and harm. If, for example, someone is refusing medication, has consideration been given to how long they are prepared to remain ill, and in all likelihood in hospital? Such an account would have to take account of episodes of acute illness not always following the same pattern with the person remaining in hospital longer than they had expected. The longer the person is ill the more likely are there to be negative consequences, including to social contacts.

The second major consideration is whether the person fully understands the consequences of their illness (in this case especially depression and mania) and understands that they could die. Compulsory treatment of patients means that this is something which rarely happens, and thus the mortality of mental illness focuses on suicide. Unless an advance statement makes it very clear that the person would rather die than accept ECT it seems likely that a psychiatrist would seek to overrule the advance statement in favour of preserving life.

The other area where mortality is likely is for people with anorexia nervosa who want to refuse artificial or force-feeding. Some psychiatrists have suggested that allowing this, even if it results in death, is a preferred option to the patient killing themselves in some other way, as is often the case (Atkinson et al., 2003b). This would be contested by Giordano (2003) who argued that anorexia should not be considered a lethal illness as its effects are reversible.

A different concern with making decisions for the future is the comparative status of the 'well' person and the 'ill' person. It raises the question of whether they are, indeed, the 'same' person or whether the 'ill' person has separate rights and should be allowed to make decisions for themselves. This is a complex philosophical problem and outwith the scope of this chapter, but has been debated elsewhere (Savulescu and Dickenson, 1998; Atkinson, in press) and in relation to loss of capacity in general (Bourgeois, 1995)

Any advance statement will be made available to the tribunal when considering a compulsory treatment order, and the tribunal has to give it due regard. It is expected that its provisions will be complied with where possible in the care plan produced and agreed at the tribunal. The code of practice suggests that if it is not possible to meet patients' wishes because services do not exist, this should be recorded in the patients' notes as an unmet need (Scottish Executive, 2005a).

Implementing an advance statement

An advance statement will come into effect when the person has lost the capacity to make decisions for themselves. In Scotland, the new impaired decision-making criterion will mean this applies to anyone subject to the MHCT Act. The focus has been on the advance statement coming into effect in relation to a CTO, but it will need to be taken account of at all periods of detention. Therefore, a check for an advance statement needs to be instigated at the start of any procedure to detain a person or compulsorily treat them.

The position of patients who are not subject to the Act is slightly less clear. There seems the have been little consideration of how advance statements might be used with people who are unable to make decisions but who do not fulfil the other criteria to be subject to the Act. The various situations that are likely to arise are shown in Figure 1.

Figure 1 Scenarios for application of advance satements

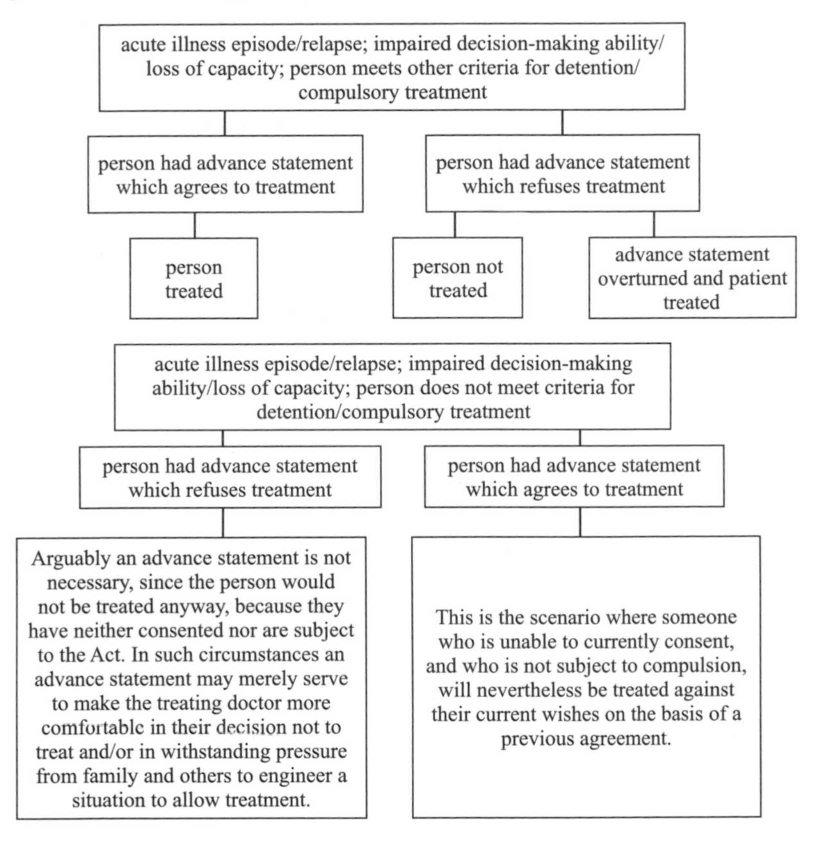

Content of advance statements

Leaving aside, for the moment, the major issues around opting in to or out of treatment, the context of advance statements can be narrow (reflecting decisions about medical treatment) or wider (taking in a range of decisions from childcare and financial matters to food preferences). In mental health care people cannot opt out of being detained.

Some users advocate very wide-ranging advance directives, covering every aspect of what they would like to happen in hospital. An example of this is given by Dace (2001) in a personal account of her attempt to use an advance directive. As well as covering treatment it included a very wide range of other requests and responses to behaviours.

This highlights the difficulty of reconciling what people would like to happen in the best of all circumstances with the practicalities of managing a wide range of individual requests with limited resources, including limited staff numbers. It is a different matter if this information is supplied as part of background information to assist clinical decisions, much like a personal statement as suggested by the Scottish Executive. Maintaining the integrity of advance statements requires a balance between on the one hand including so many demands that inevitably they will not or cannot be met, and on the other being so limited in scope that they constrain patients' choice.

Although it might be assumed that people making an advance directive without the input of staff are more likely to make conditions which cannot be upheld, this may not always be the case. An advance directive in the form of a 'Preference of Care' booklet was completed, in London, by patients in conjunction with a staff member. The top response for what people did not want to happen in response to becoming ill again was 'force/coercion/intrusion' (43%) (Papageorgiou et al., 2002, 2004). If this implies that they want to opt out of the provisions of the Mental Health Act, or not feel coerced because its use is a possibility, then was this a reasonable choice for people to make (or to allow people to make), when in fact they do not have that choice? Sixteen per cent did not want to be admitted by staff unknown to them, again something which, though desirable, may prove practically impossible. Likewise, 43% said that what they did want was 'better quality hospital facilities'. While this might be a legitimate and completely understandable wish it is unlikely that it can be achieved through an advance directive. Other requests were for alternative therapies, counselling and psychotherapy, requested by 33%; and 'improved human rights', requested by 32%. Who is responsible for complying with such requests is not clear, nor is how these relate to resource issues. If this Preference for Care booklet had been a legally binding document, it is all too clear what problems would have been created. Such preferences may have contributed to its lack of use.

For those concerned that the advent of advance statements will lead to large numbers of patients refusing treatment, this does not seem to be borne out in practice. In the Papageorgiou et al. study (2004), only 15% were refusing a particular treatment at hospital admission, compared with 25% who wanted 'support to take medication' if they became ill again.

Elsewhere there are similar findings. In Oregon, USA, 40 patients with 'severe and persistent mental disorders' completed a legally sanctioned psychiatric advance directive (PAD). In no case did a patient refuse all treatment, although ECT was refused by 57% and the drug haloperidol was specifically refused by 27% (Backlar et al., 2001).

Other aspects of advance directives which do not have to do with treatment nevertheless stem directly from the person's illness and symptoms. Thus people who become manic may want measures put in place to stop them spending money, or engaging in sexual behaviour they consider inappropriate or other behaviours which they believe will damage them. Who is to take responsibility for this is not easy to determine. Can psychiatrists, for example, confiscate someone's credit card? In one study, nurses were clear that they did not want to be responsible for custody of patients' credit cards (Atkinson et al., 2003b) Controlling a person's sexual activity may mean not only hospitalising them but keeping a very close watch on them in hospital. It may be that some of these interventions are best carried out by family members or friends, and plans agreed between the person, family and clinical team are the best approach. Whoever is to take charge, the parameters have to be laid down very clearly. One person's extravagant spending may seem reasonable to another.

In these examples it is also likely that the intervention will have to come before there is clear evidence that the person has lost capacity. Spending more than x amount per week may be a guide, but may still not prevent one large spending spree. Preventing unwanted sexual behaviour may be even more problematic since it is likely that the person wants to prevent the first unwanted encounter as much as subsequent ones.

Storage and availability of advance statements

A crucial requirement of an advance directive is that it is immediately available when required. In theory the provisions made under the MCHT should mean that there is no difficulty in locating a copy. Research elsewhere, however, has suggested that they are not always found or used. Care plans, similar to advance directives, placed in the front of a patient's notes were often ignored (Papageorgiou et al., 2002, 2004). An advantage with the Scottish law is that there are multiple copies and, more importantly, the tribunal will have a duty to ask whether an advance statement exists.

Activating an advance directive

The problem in activating an advance directive which is not triggered by the use of mental health legislation is that somebody has to raise the question of the patient's capacity, and somebody, usually the psychiatrist, will have to formally assess capacity and record this in the patient's notes. This is something psychiatrists generally seem loath to do, and is not usually part of current practice.

For both joint crisis plans and the Preference for Care booklet (Henderson et al., 2004; Papageorgeiou et al 2002, 2004) there was no clear indication of when they would come into force other than the person becoming ill again. It was not clear that the question of capacity was being formally addressed. This might not be an issue if the person remains content with the decisions previously agreed, but it is likely to cause problems if they have changed their mind. A person who retains capacity cannot be held to a previously agreed decision if they now want to refuse consent. This may be further complicated if one intention of having the crisis plan is to avoid the use of the Mental Health Act. Although in many ways this can be a very positive outcome, it also means that patients do not have the various safeguards which come with being treated under the Act.

There is a potential problem if crisis plans and the like are equated with advance directives. Crisis plans are what they say – plans to manage circumstances when the patient is ill and in crisis. This does not mean that the person has always lost capacity. Advance directives are very clearly designed to be implemented when the person no longer has the capacity to make a decision. This is more than a matter of semantics. When a person becomes acutely ill, to invoke an advance directive without a formal assessment of capacity looks as though being acutely ill is the same as lacking capacity. The 1983 and 1984 Mental Health Acts have never assumed this, and the MHCT Act only allows for impaired medical decision-making. It would be a retrograde step if the promotion of advance directives led to the assumption that all people who are acutely mentally ill are not able to take part in making competent decisions at the time.

The impact of advance directives

Although it might be reasonable to ask what impact using advance directives has, or even what the outcome is, this is not a straightforward question, which may partly explain why there are few studies in this area. What should the impact be? In part this will depend on whose perspective is taken and in particular on the type of advance directive involved.

Patients may be more interested in whether things work out as they hoped than anything else. An advance directive might be complied with but the consequences may be unexpected or not what was intended. Simply recording whether or not an advance directive was complied with or overruled would not answer this question.

Clinical and service providers are likely to have an interest in how the advance directive impacts on the use of services. This will take in the patient's clinical state. The easiest outcomes to measure will be admission to hospital, time spent in hospital and the use of the Mental Health Act. Changes to treatment and care from what would normally have been provided is another approach, but would only be appropriate for advance directives which were made independently of the treating doctor. Co-operative agreements will produce a care plan which could be deemed optimal in the circumstances.

These approaches are problematic in that they take no account of the intention of the advance directive, or those involved may be looking for different outcomes. Thus a patient may be prepared to accept both a hospital admission and a longer period in hospital if it means that they do not have to take medication: they may thus see the advance directive as successful, whereas a clinician or hospital manager, hard-pressed to find a bed, may view this outcome as negative.

Carers and family members may have yet another perspective. Many are likely to be unhappy with a clinician who complies with an advance directive which refuses treatment, leaving their relative ill and in distress, especially if they remain at home. A survey of various stakeholders in the USA suggested that other benefits which might come from having an advance directive might be reducing stigma or promoting responsibility in patients (Backlar et al., 2001).

As a result, various research methodologies and outcomes will need to be employed to assess the impact of advance directives. They should include some quantitative evidence of use, type of conditions/content, number overruled and why, impact on hospital admission and stay, and use of legislation. These are in addition to the qualitative studies required, looking at the impact of the advance directive/statement on both patients and professionals, and their perspective on it. This might include considering whether patients and doctors have a better understanding of each other as a result of discussions in drawing up agreements.

Two randomised trials of forms of advance directive in London looked at compulsory admission as the main outcome measure (Papageorgiou et al., 2002, 2004, Henderson et al., 2004). That they came to apparently contradictory conclusions adds to the confusion surrounding outcomes.

The first study (Papageorgiou et al., 2002, 2004) used the previously mentioned Preference for Care booklet, which was completed with an 'independent' member of staff at the time when patients were about to be discharged from compulsory treatment. The booklet contained the statement that 'professionals were not legally bound to comply with the stated preferences. One hundred and fifty-six patients were randomised to either this new approach or a control group following standard care and procedures. It is not clear when the booklet was used, but it seems that it was as the patient became ill again rather than when capacity was lost. Follow-up over 12 months indicated that on re-admission to hospital under a section of the Mental Health Act there was no significant difference between the groups in the number of patients with a voluntary admission to hospital or the number of days spent in hospital.

This was in contrast to a study of joint crisis plans (Henderson et al., 2004) which the authors noted were not advance directives as such because they were fully agreed with staff. In this study, 160 patients were randomised to developing and agreeing a joint crisis plan with staff. A control group received standard treatment plus leaflets on the Mental Health Act (1983) treatment and relevant policies. The patients all had a psychotic illness or a non-psychotic bi-polar illness, had been inpatients in the last two years and were in contact with services. Significantly fewer of the crisis plan group than the control group were being compulsorily treated under the Mental Health Act. For patients who were admitted under the Act there was no difference between the groups in the number of days they were detained, nor was there a difference in the number of days spent as an inpatient. The difference in the use of the Act was found despite 15 of the 80 patients in the intervention group not having a crisis plan.

Are these findings really contradictory or do they report on different types of plans/advance directives, with different types of patients compared at different times? In practical terms might these things have made little difference? Both studies seem to have been compromised to a certain degree by lack of staff co-operation. In the Henderson et al. study, in 8 of the 15 cases without a crisis plan this was because of lack of co-operation by staff. In looking at psychiatrists' views on using the Preference for Care booklet, Papageorgiou et al. (2004) only had responses for 39% of patients with only 3 psychiatrists reporting using it. Despite it being placed at the front of the patient's notes there seems to have been low awareness of its existence. Fifteen per cent (9 out of 59) patients indicated that the Preference for Care booklet had been helpful, although 41% optimistically reported that they would want to use it again. These findings would suggest that little notice was taken off the Preference for Care booklet and therefore it is not surprising that it did not have an impact.

These studies also raise the question whether a randomised controlled trial is the best way to evaluate the impact and outcomes of advance directives. These are not interventions as such; they are ways of allowing people to take responsibility for the management of their illness or exert their choice of how it is managed. To expect them to deliver any particular kind of standard outcome may not make any sense.

The future of advance statements

How advance statements come to be used in Scotland and the impact they have will depend on a number of things. Of most importance is how much they are taken up and used by those for whom they are most suited. Talking to people in the USA, where they have been available for a time, suggests that it is only a small minority of patients who actually make them. Research studies might improve take-up and present a slightly skewed picture. A study in Washington State indicated that 53% of a sample of patients who were high users of crisis services and hospital admission were interested in making an advance directive (Srebnik et al., 2003). Only 8% of those who gave a reason said that it was because they wanted to plan for a time when they lacked capacity. The two main reasons (27% each) were that their case managers had suggested it or they believed it would be useful. The two characteristics of patients that were significantly related to wanting to make an advance directive were not having an outpatient commitment order and having the support of their case manager. This would suggest that take-up in Scotland might be enhanced if advance statements are promoted by staff involved in patients' care and patients are given advice and support in how to make one.

Something which may contribute to take-up in Scotland is that advance statements have been introduced as part of new legislation which covers the entire country. All staff will be aware of these changes and their responsibility to check for advance statements, so some of the problems encountered in the London studies, for example, should be avoided. Patients who are, or have been, subject to the previous Mental Health Act are likely to be aware of changes. The extensive consultation carried out before the new Act, and the efforts put into promoting initiatives such as advance statements, hopefully mean that knowledge of these has reached a large number of people for whom they may be relevant. Also, because their existence has to be checked for at the time of detention, knowledge of them should eventually reach the most appropriate group of patients.

A cautionary note needs to be sounded over equating take-up of advance statements with their success. In the targeted study in Washington State, nearly half did not want to make an advance directive. This does not mean that the programme itself is unsuccessful, and the reasons why patients are not interested in advance directives even when they might be seen to be an appropriate group need to be explored.

Although some people may be happy with the treatment they receive, and the plans made, not everyone who does not want to make an advance directive may be in this position. People may not be satisfied with their current treatment but will not want to make an advance directive. These reasons need to be explored. Some may be:

- denial of current mental illness or the possibility of becoming ill again (e.g. the 19% in Srebnik et al., 2003);
- satisfaction with plans to manage future episodes/crisis (17% in Srebnik et al., 2003);
- continuation of current treatment (20% in Backlar et al., 2001);
- no faith that an advance directive will be implemented and therefore there is no point in making one;
- what is wanted is not available on the NHS (e.g. some alternative

treatment) or is not allowed in an advance directive (e.g. opting out of being detained);

- to make an advance directive is too upsetting or too challenging as it means facing up to the (almost certain) inevitability of future crises. (This is not the same as the first reason, as in this case the likelihood is accepted, but the person prefers to maintain a more 'hopeful' stance.) This may include patients who, despite a major illness have not been subject to the Mental Health Act.

Thus not everyone who does not make an advance directive can be assumed to be happy with the status quo, but neither should there be an assumption that all patients are unhappy with the treatment they receive.

Advance statements are not a treatment intervention; there is no clear consensus on whether they 'work' or, indeed, even what 'works' really means. It is unlikely to be appropriate to expect (or even try to ensure) that all patients with a recurring mental illness make one. For such reasons we need to look more closely in Scotland at why they are useful where patients and/or psychiatrists believe them to be, and how best to proceed with implementing options for people who are not happy with their current and/or proposed future treatment but do not want to make an advance statement.

CHAPTER 5

The Involvement of Relatives

It is now appreciated that relatives, and to a lesser extent friends, play a part in caring for people with a major mental illness, and the need to provide support and services for them is accepted. They are also included or consulted in planning and policy matters. This was less the case when Sir Roy Griffith reported to the Thatcher government on community care (Griffith, 1988). Although there was at that time an acknowledgment that such carers played a major part in caring for ill relatives, and were therefore the cornerstone of the new NHS and Community Care Act 1990, their role and relationship were somewhat taken for granted. A case had repeatedly to be made for acknowledging their role and contribution and the need to support them in this (Atkinson and Coia, 1989, 1991).

Organisations of relatives or carers have gradually proliferated across the globe since the National Schizophrenia Fellowship started in the UK in 1972 (Atkinson and Coia, 1995). Services are now provided for carers as well as for the 'patient', so that both of them are now service users and there is sometimes ambiguity in respect of their roles (Atkinson and Coia, 1995). While many relatives/carers are the mainstay of their ill relative, advocate on their behalf and selflessly support them, this is not true of all carers. This needs to be borne in mind in any reform of the law. Legislation should not make the assumption that all relatives act in their ill relative's best interest.

Indeed, abuse by relatives was a main focus of the earliest legislation specifically to do with mental health in Britain, the Act for Regulating Private Madhouses 1774. The Act policed the management of the 'mad' and aimed to stop relatives and proprietors of madhouses colluding to incarcerate relatives. This could happen in various circumstances, but of particular concern was the incarceration of wealthy but unstable relatives which gave others access to, and control of, their money and land. With no records, even of transfer between institutions, unscrupulous and greedy relatives were able to ensure that their troublesome relatives disappeared. The Act seemed at least as interested in protecting property rights as it did in inappropriate incarceration. The Act, however, had no real enforcement powers and was therefore largely ignored.

Later legislation regulated the building of, and conditions in, asylums.

Although there is no doubt that conditions often were appalling and remained so (Parry-Jones, 1972; Scull, 1982; Porter, 1990), other historians of psychiatry have suggested that asylums were set up to protect the mad from the inhuman conditions in which they were living with their family or in the community (Jones, 1991; Shorter, 1997). Commentators at the time described not only the conditions in asylums but also the squalor of the conditions of the day (Chadwick, 1842; Dix, 1843).

Review of the relative's role

The specific role of 'nearest relative' was introduced in the Mental Health Act 1959 in England and Wales and 1960 in Scotland, following on from the review of the previous Act by the Percy Commission (1957). Although at the time it was believed unlikely that a reasonable or responsible relative (or social worker) would go against the advice and recommendations of a doctor, there was also agreement that provision must be made for this contingency.

The revision of the laws in the early 1980s developed and extended the powers of the nearest relative. They were defined under the Acts and equated to what most people would think of as next-of-kin. The role of nearest relative applied to rights and responsibilities under mental health legislation in relation to formal admission and discharge. The person had to be over 18 years (unless a spouse or parent) and resident in the UK. There were rules relating to divorce, separation and partnerships, full and half-blood relationships and residence. Age was a consideration, with the eldest in a category (e.g. eldest child, eldest sibling) taking precedence. Where there was no nearest relative (or they were unable or unwilling to act) a person could apply to the sheriff court (in Scotland) to become the nearest relative. An opposite-sex partner could be treated as a spouse after six months, but same-sex partners had to have cohabited for five years. This referred to the provision for the person to live with any non-relative for at least five years before they could be treated as the nearest relative. The rule regarding same-sex partners was changed to that of opposite-sex partners, following a court action in Liverpool (*R.* v. *Liverpool City Council* [2002]).

The nearest relative had a range of rights, including the right to receive information if the person was detained; to consent to emergency or short-term detention; to apply to a sheriff court to have the patient detained, or to request a MHO to do this; to be heard at court and call witnesses; to request an independent psychiatric examination; to discharge, or apply for discharge for, a detained patient; and to be told about renewal of detention, which they could then appeal against in the sheriff court. The nearest relative could thus act as an advocate for the patient, in terms of either what they believed to be in the patient's best interest or what they thought the patient themselves would do. In these terms the nearest relative can be seen as a safeguard for the patient. It is also clear that problems would have existed where the nearest relative did not have the patient's best interests in mind and could use their potential powers against the patient's current or previously expressed wishes.

The review of the Acts in both countries revealed a number of problem areas. There was almost no real research on the nearest relative and how the provisions were working. There are some unpublished theses and reports (e.g. Carter, 1999; Gregor, 1999; Summers et al., 2000) and one substantial published piece of work (Rapaport, 2004, 2005).

Case law in England has highlighted some problems with the nearest relative role, particularly the problem of removing an unsuitable relative, and this has weakened their position. This problem had been highlighted by the Mental Health Act Commission (1991), which recommended that the criteria governing the displacement of an unsuitable nearest relative should be revised. Two cases brought by patients alleging sexual abuse by their relatives (*JT* v. *United Kingdom* 26494/95 and *FC* v. *United Kingdom* 37344/97) were finally won under the Human Rights Act 1998 (cited in Rapaport, 2004). The European Court of Human Rights found that the nearest relative provisions in British law were in breach of Article 8, which upholds the right to respect for private and family life. As a consequence of this the government pledged, in a 'friendly' out-of-court settlement with JT, to change the law to allow patients to change their nearest relative under reasonable circumstances. This has still not happened in England and Wales, pending the review of the legislation in its entirety.

This has again been raised in *R. (on the application of M)* v. *Secretary of State for Health* [2003] EWHC (Admin) (16 April 2003) (reported by Rapaport, 2004). It is possible for an approved social worker (ASW, the equivalent in England and Wales of the MHO in Scotland) to displace an inappropriate nearest relative, but the procedures are long and complex and a disincentive to the ASW to act (Rapaport, 2004). Another case has also weakened the nearest relative role. The delay that had often surrounded the displacement of an allegedly inappropriate nearest relative who was objecting to powers under the Act such as treatment or guardianship orders, or who was wanting to discharge a patient, was effectively stopped following *R.* v. *Central London County Court ex parte Ax London* [1999] 2 All ER 991 (Rapaport, 2004, 2005).

For patients who were detained under criminal justice sections of the Act, the role of nearest relative carries no legal powers, as was clarified in R v Mental Health Review tribunal ex parte H [2000] All ER (D) 2189 (Rapaport 2004).

Consultation in the review had led to an awareness of other problems with the position of named relative. One issue was that of the relationship between nearest relative and primary carer. In many cases a patient's nearest relative was also their main carer, but not in all. In some cases, the main carer – the person who took most responsibility for care and support of the patent

– did not have any rights, while the nearest relative – someone who might not be involved, or who might be actively antagonistic to the patient – did, and was able to override the carer simply because of closer blood ties. The Millan Committee, and many others, felt this was unfair, as well as having implications for care.

The study on the position of nearest relative under the 1983 Act in England and Wales (Rapaport, 2004) includes accounts of antagonistic relationships where the nearest relative used their position to further their own ends, including seeking custody of children or proceeding with separation or divorce arrangements. There was a need, therefore, to look at the nearest relative concept from the position of care and support rather than mere biology.

Another concern raised about the nearest relative's role was the part played in the admission to hospital under the 1983 Act. Where practicable, a relative, rather than an MHO or ASW, could consent to emergency or short-term detention. Although originally intended as a safeguard, this provision was not generally viewed as such. Both relatives and patients found the role difficult and distressing and saw it as leading to difficulties in their relationship. Relatives could feel guilty, blaming themselves for having their relative 'put way' or 'sectioned', and they could be blamed by the patient. Relatives' and patients' lack of knowledge of their rights meant that some have found themselves 'forced' to act against their inclination (Rapaport, 2004).

A study in South Glasgow from April 1997 to March 1998 showed that for detention under the civil sections of the 1984 Act, in 42% of the cases consent was provided by relatives (Taylor and Idris, 2003). If relatives no longer have a role in consenting to admission under the Act the work of MHOs will have to increase to take up this shortfall. Relatives are frequently supportive of their ill relative, accompanying them to hospital (Taylor et al., 1996). This role can remain intact while removing the formal requirements.

Despite policy and some service changes, many relatives still complained that their views and wishes were not taken into account when care packages were planned, and that if they are expected to take responsibility, then they should be accorded some rights (Rapaport, 2004).

The Millan Committee made a number of recommendations regarding the role of carers and relatives, the major one being the replacement of the nearest relative with the introduction of the 'named person'. Some groups had wanted wider consideration of carers, although it is reflected in the principles:

> The Millan Committee said a lot about carers, but that is not fully reflected in the Bill. The named person is included, but primary carers, informal carers and other members of the family who are carers are not. If they were included, the MHO would have to consult more than one carer when undertaking their social circumstances

> report. Although MHOs may do so at the moment they should be required to do so. (Jeanette Gardner, National Schizophrenia Fellowship (Scotland), in Scottish Parliament, 2002e, col. 3229)

And later:

> There are three places in the bill where, I think, the primary carer might be mentioned along with the named person. Stating a principle about carers in the bill is essential. (Jeanette Gardner, National Schizophrenia Fellowship (Scotland), in Scottish Parliament, 2002e, col. 3242)

Named person

The new role of named person is introduced in section 250 of the MHCT Act. The main purpose of this person is to safeguard the rights of the patient who is subject to the Act. It is described in *A Guide to Named Persons* (Scottish Executive, 2004c) thus:

> A named person can help to protect your interests if you have to be given care or treatment under the new Act. Under the new Act you can have a named person who will have to be informed and consulted about aspects of your care, and who can make certain applications (p. 4).

The named person has certain rights under the Act. These are:

- to be consulted in defined circumstances (for example, when an application for a CTO is being made); or
- when certain changes in circumstances are made (for example, when a short-term order is revoked);
- to receive certain records and information given to the patient, including notification of treatment given which is contrary to a valid advance statement;
- to make an application or appeal to the MHTS, and to speak at, or lead evidence at, a tribunal hearing;
- to consent, where the patient is unable so to do, to two medical examinations taking place at the same time (for example, where these are needed for an application for a CTO);
- to request a needs assessment for the patient from the local authority and/or the health board.

These rights are considerable and should be taken into account by the patient when nominating a named person.

Named persons only have rights when a patient is subject to the MHCT Act. If a person is a voluntary (or 'informal') patient, the named person has no rights. Anyone involved in the care of a person being treated under the

Act has to take account of the views of the named person, as well as the patient's past and present wishes.

Named persons and patients act independently of each other, and there is no requirement for an agreed course of action. Named persons can act independently, for example by applying to the tribunal for review without consulting the patient or the patient requesting this. *A Guide to Named Persons* (Scottish Executive, 2004c) therefore suggests that 'you will want to choose someone who knows you well and whom you trust to act in your best interests'.

'Best interest' is not usually taken to mean the same as 'substituted judgement', which will be discussed briefly later. It is suggested, however, that if a named person always acted in contravention of the patient's expressed wishes, this might be a good reason for either the patient or another appropriate person seeking to have them displaced.

Any competent adult (i.e. over 16 years) can choose who they want for their named person, although the chosen person has to agree to the role. If the person does not want to appoint a named person (or if the person named is not willing to act as such), the person's main carer is automatically the named person. If there is more than one adult carer, they decide who will be the named person. If the person has no adult carer willing to act, then the nearest relative (as defined in the Act) becomes the named person. Where there is no nearest relative willing or able to be the named person, then the person's MHO, or anyone else with an interest in the person's welfare, can apply to the MHTS with a request that someone be appointed the patient's named person. Although a patient can make a 'declaration' to prevent a particular person being appointed as their named person, and the tribunal has to take the patient's wishes into account, it does have the power to appoint whomsoever it deems fit.

Anyone who is over the age of 16, who understands what is involved and who agrees, can be a named person. However, because the named person has to be able to act independently in the patient's best interests, they should not be someone who has any professional responsibility for providing care. Nor should the named person be an independent advocate, as these are distinct roles and an individual cannot act in both roles at the same time.

Patients can also revoke their nomination for their named person. As in nominating a named person, the person's competency to revoke the nomination has to be witnessed. There is a form of words available.[1] It is possible for others to apply to the Tribunal to have a patient's named person changed. Although five categories of people are named (responsible medical officer, hospital managers for inpatients, welfare attorney, guardian and relatives) a catch-all clause 'anyone else who has an interest in the patient's welfare' makes the list largely redundant.

Professionals may choose to oppose a nominated person for a variety of reasons, but are likely to focus on concern that the named person may not act in the patient's best interest – which may include evidence or suspicion of bullying, coercion or abuse – or concern for the privacy of the patient and the use that might be made of information to which the named person would have a right.

Any of the documents nominating or changing a named person must be witnessed by someone from a prescribed list. These are a doctor, a registered nurse, a solicitor, a social worker, a clinical psychologist, or an occupational therapist. These people have to assert that the person is capable of making the decision – in this case taken to mean that the person understands the effect of the decision – and that the decision has been made freely, without undue pressure. Some of these people may charge for their time to act as a witness. For solicitors legal aid may be available.

Although forms are suggested by the Scottish Executive, the law does not require these to be used. Nor is there a requirement to register nominations or revocations, although clearly this would be sensible. It is likely that a few people may change their minds on a fairly frequent basis or make multiple nominations without always revoking a previous nomination. In such cases it will be difficult for the MHO to be sure who is the appropriate named person.

Children under 16 cannot choose a named person. The named person is automatically their parent or guardian (and who is over 16), failing whom the child's main carer (who is over 16). There is no provision for this to be declined. If the child is under a care order under the Children Act 1989, then the local authority will act as the named person. These arrangements caused some concern and safeguards were looked for:

> On balance, we support the system of automatically assigning a parent to be the named person, because a child's situation is different from an adult's, but it is critical that that can be challenged in a tribunal ... Although, of course, most parents are working in the best interests of their child, there are circumstances in which that will not happen – obviously, there might be tie-ups between the child's mental health problems and those of their parents. That is why strong protections must be included in the legislation. (Kay Tisdall, Children in Scotland, in Scottish Parliament, 2002g, col. 3318)

Franks and Cobb (2005) suggest that section 256 would appear to allow a patient who is under the age of 16 to apply to the Tribunal regarding a named person, although unable to do so under section 250.

A named person will only be able to function if people know who the person is, and similar considerations apply as to the dissemination of an advance statement. At the very least, those involved in care and treatment will need to know – the responsible medical officer, GP, MHO, CPN, solicitor (if the person has one), independent advocate (if the person has one), and also carers and relatives.

Balancing the rights of the patient and the named person

There is an inherent paradox in the role of the named person: they act as a safeguard for the patient but, because of their considerable rights, including to information, they are also in a position to learn more about the patient than they, the patient, might want. There are some causes for concern. Medical information – which may include a medical history or reference to past events – given to the named person may divulge things about which they knew nothing and about which the patient may want them to remain in ignorance. For example, the patient's history may include abuse or events such as abortion, which the patient may not want divulged.

Although in theory a person is free to nominate anyone as their named person, in practice this may not be so easy. Where there is a spouse or partner, an individual may feel obliged to appoint that person as their named person or risk problems with the relationship. They may choose this person even if they know the nominated person would make choices they would not. The same issue might also exist with other main carers, where there would be an assumption that they would 'naturally' be the named person. Although the Act distinguishes between named person and primary carer, it is likely that for many people it will be appropriate for this to be one and the same person. It is where the patient is not happy with this, or sees a conflict in roles, that difficulties may arise. An individual may not feel able, for example, not to appoint their spouse or partner even if they do not think this person will act in their best interest, and would prefer, say, their child. Similarly, an adult child may not want their parent, but may still live with that parent (often through lack of other available, appropriate accommodation) and may feel unable to appoint someone else. It may be that in these circumstances a professional could act on behalf of the patient to remove a named person and thus deflect any resultant emotion away from the patient.

As mentioned earlier, the guidance from the Scottish Executive (2004c) indicates that the named person should act in the patient's 'best interest'. This is a commonly used expression, but its meaning is open to interpretation. Essentially it is based on the fundamental ethical principle of beneficence, that is, doing good, but it can very easily take on a paternalistic mantle. It is usually seen as being based on taking decisions in an emergency or other 'necessary' situations, which are usually deemed to be life-threatening. In most cases preservation of life is seen as in the person's best interest. In mental illness, however, 'necessary' does not always mean preserving life. Very often in such cases it means treating the illness to prevent deterioration and/or improve the quality of the person's life. In such circumstances best interest may appropriately be defined more widely. It could thus take in past and current wishes of the patient, the views of significant other people in the person's life and the principle of least restrictive alternative (Wong and Clare, 1999). It has already been noted that least restrictive alternative could be interpreted as acting on the competently expressed wishes of the person, for example through an advance statement (Atkinson and Garner, 2002).

The concerns about the named person notwithstanding, it is likely that for the majority of patients having a supportive, freely chosen named person will be seen as an important safeguard. Only time, supported by monitoring and research, will tell whether the named person role provides the safeguards intended.

Nearest relative

Where a named person has not been appointed, the nearest relative may be consulted. This would be particularly important, for example, in a first episode, when the question of a named person has not previously arisen. The Act sets out a hierarchy of nearest relatives in which the spouse takes precedence (unless permanently separated). The Act gives equal weight to opposite-sex and same-sex partnerships, where a cohabitee of at least six months is the nearest relative in the absence of a spouse. A person who has lived with another for at least five years can be regarded as the nearest relative if there is no one else higher in the hierarchy.

If a patient becomes subject to an emergency detention, the nearest relative must be informed. If they do not live with the patient then someone who does live with them must be informed. Clearly there is a need to establish a person's whereabouts and prevent any anxiety that someone is missing.

Carers

Representation was made during consultation before and during the progress of the bill, arguing for carers (informal and usually relatives) to be taken into account more, and a number of amendments were submitted to that end. Putting this into practice, however, was always going to be problematic unless carers were specified in some way in the Act. A general requirement to inform or consult 'carers' (beyond the primary carer) could lead to problems where one person defined themselves as a carer, but others, including other carers and/or the patient, did not. Without a definitive list an MHO or psychiatrist could never be certain that everyone who believed themselves entitled to be consulted had been.

As well as the question of balance between patients' rights (including privacy and confidentiality) and carers' rights or expectations, there are also practical aspects to consider. Time-scales in the Act have to be kept as tight as possible to protect patients from unacceptable delays and inappropriate detention, but also need to be long enough for the work for applications to be carried out appropriately (which is also in the patient's interests) and with consideration for other workload issues. Carers can, or course, give evidence at a tribunal hearing.

The Act does not deal with the issue of carers who are children, and services will have to be alert and sensitive to this.

Note

1. The forms/wording to be used in making a declaration or otherwise revoking a nomination are given in the Scottish Executive's *A Guide to Named Persons*, (available online at www.scotland.gov.uk/Publications/2004/10/20016/44075). Such declarations must be witnessed.

Chapter 6

Legislation and the Changing Face of Service Delivery

Part 4 of the Act sets out the duties of health boards and local authorities to provide certain services. Health boards and local authorities had two and a half years to prepare for the implementation of the Act, but when it was implemented in October 2005 it was not clear that they had all had responded appropriately on all aspects. The Scottish Executive maintained a monitoring brief over the progress made by health boards through the joint local implementation planning (JLIP) procedures. Eleven delivery indicators were outlined:

- tribunal;
- human resources;
- crisis response and 24-hour services;
- perinatal mental health services;
- age-sensitive (under age 18) inpatient care and accommodation;
- advocacy;
- local authority functions;
- appeals against levels of security (for implementation by May 2006);
- learning disability;
- Joint Future;
- other issues.

Oddly, some matters such as named person and advance statements only appeared under the indicator for learning disability, when they clearly apply to all people.

These plans were updated regularly. Up-to-date information can be accessed on the web (www.show.scot.nhs.uk/mhwbsg/jlip/home.htm).

An assessment of mental health services' ability to meet the demands of the new Act was commissioned by the Scottish Executive. The aim was to map existing services, thus enabling the identification of gaps, duplications and shortcomings in quality as well as quantity of services; and to review the available evidence regarding the organisation, management, efficiency and effectiveness of services. These were assessed against the needs of the new Act and suggestions to be made regarding priority service development. The final report (Grant, 2004a, b) highlighted areas for improvement and recommendations. These ranged from changing staff attitudes to workforce shortages and service delivery. Particularly highlighted were the need for 24-hour crisis support in the community; local hospital admission (except for specialist services); higher quality accommodation geared to individual needs (especially age-appropriate accommodation, mother and baby units and accommodation for mentally disordered offenders) and a range of therapies including psychosocial interventions, daytime activities and employment and support for recovery. Throughout there was an emphasis not just on health services and local authorities working together but also on including voluntary organisations, service users and carers.

This chapter cannot look in detail at services and all the developments expected in service provision, but now considers briefly the new duties on health boards to provide age-appropriate services and services for women with post-natal depression, and the new requirements for local authorities. The need to take account of the underlying principles such as reciprocity will also impact on services, and concern has been expressed about the development of a two-tier system of care. Lastly, some brief consideration will be given to workforce issues in all services. One area not dealt with because of space, but which requires consideration in service delivery, is that of culturally sensitive services and the needs of minority ethnic and other groups.

Services for children and young people

Health boards have to provide age-appropriate services for children and young persons under the age of 18 (section 23), whether as a voluntary or detained patient. This follows a scathing denouncement of child and adolescent mental health services to both the Millan Committee and the Parliamentary Committee:

> Our facilities for adolescent in-patients in Scotland are a national disgrace. (Dr Denise Coia, Royal College of Psychiatrists, in Scottish Parliament, 2002e, col. 3214)

At the time there were 34 beds, although the recommended number for a population of 5 million was 80–100 beds. In earlier testimony Dr Coia had reported on adolescents being inappropriately admitted to adult wards as:

> a frightening and distressing experience ... A very disturbed adult unit, often with violent and aggressive male patients, is not the place to be at that point in time. We would very much welcome a duty of care. (Dr Denise Coia, Royal College of Psychiatrists, in Scottish Parliament, 2002b, col. 3096)

A report from the Royal College of Psychiatrists (2002) said that children under the age of 16 should not be admitted to adult wards and that special circumstances are necessary before admission is appropriate for 16- and 17-year-olds. It suggested that inappropriate admissions to such wards should be treated as an 'untoward critical incident'. In 2005 the Mental Welfare Commission described the practice as 'deeply undesirable and may be harmful to the young person' (Mental Welfare Commission for Scotland, 2005b).

In 1995–6 there were 82 episodes of detention of young people under 18 in Scotland, rising to 135 in 2003–4 and 166 in 2004–5 (Mental Welfare Commission for Scotland, 1996, 2004, 2005a). This represented a 27% increase in the past twelve months. The biggest increase was in 16-17 year olds. There were 29 detentions of children under 16, an increase of 7% (or two children).

It is difficult to get good figures on young people admitted to adult mental health wards as this tends to rely on health services notifying the Mental Welfare Commission of voluntary admissions. Also, the Mental Welfare Commission does not always report the same statistics. In 2003–4, of the 135 young people detained only 20 (15%) were in child and adolescent units, 106 (70%) were on adult mental health wards and nine (7%) were on medical wards. This includes five 16–17–year-olds admitted to adult wards under the Criminal Procedures (Scotland) Act 1995 (Mental Welfare Commission for Scotland, 2004). The 2004–5 annual report only gives figures for those under 16. Of the 29 detentions of those under 16, eight (28%) were admitted to adult mental health wards. The Mental Welfare Commission also reported that it knew of seven informal admissions of people under 16 to adult mental health wards, and that this was likely to be an underestimate. The Commission did not know how many have been admitted informally to paediatric wards (Mental Welfare Commission for Scotland, 2005a). As a result of their concern they have produced practice guidance on the admission to adult wards of those under 18 (Mental Welfare Commission for Scotland, 2005b).

A report on child and adolescent mental health services by the Scottish Needs Assessment Programme (SNAP) was published in 2003. It suggested that the need for investment in specialist units in Scotland was urgent, and that the ongoing practice of admitting children and young people to adult wards – where they had not been adapted to meet the child's needs – was unacceptable. Following this a draft framework was put out for consultation on promotion, prevention and care issues in children and young people's mental health. The draft was generally greeted warmly, but it was noted that a few respondents thought the focus on 'the improving mental health agenda' was at the expense of severe and enduring mental health problems in children and young people, including attention deficit hyperactivity disorder (ADHD) and autistic spectrum disorder (ASD). There was also concern about the lack of involvement with learning disability (Phin, 2005).

This was followed by the framework document (Scottish Executive, 2005g). That it was signed by both Lewis Macdonald, the Deputy Minister for Health and Community Care, and Robert Brown, the Deputy Minister for Education and Young People, was an indication of the importance of taking a broad approach to mental health needs of children and young people.

The framework's final chapter, on specialist child and adolescent mental health services, laid out 17 service elements with indicators of activity required and outcomes expected. These were:

- planning and commissioning;
- generic teams of mental health practitioners specialising in work with children and young people across the care pathway;
- emergency and out-of-hours mental health arrangements;
- intensive outreach services;
- inpatient psychiatric services;
- primary mental health work;
- early intervention (in terms of both life-cycle and 'the problem cycle');
- liaison with secondary health care settings;
- children and young people with complex physical disorders;
- children and young people with learning disability and mental health problems;
- forensic services;
- substance misuse;
- liaison with services for looked after and accommodated children and young people;
- therapeutic services;
- staff training and development;
- clinical effectiveness;
- research and development.

The Mental Welfare Commission has produced practice guidance on the admission to adult wards for those under 18 (Mental Welfare Commission for Scotland, 2005b).

Despite the lead time into the Act, not all health boards had considered the best way of providing age-appropriate care for children and young people. The Mental Welfare Commission expressed concern about this, along with the need for 'additional funding to achieve the recommendations' (Mental Welfare Commission for Scotland, 2005a). The Commission believed that:

> Given the current state of services, we think it is unrealistic to expect that, in the immediate future, everybody under 18 who requires admission can be treated in an appropriate children's or

> young people's unit. (Mental Welfare Commission for Scotland, 2005a, p. 62)

Some attention has been given to young people with a psychotic illness and to the suggestion that there should be special services for those aged between 15 and 22 who have a psychotic illness, rather than placing them in a general child and adolescent unit (Calton and Arcelus, 2003; Mears et al., 2003). This relates not just to experiences of staff treating the young person but also to the impact of psychotic or other distressing behaviour on children on the ward. White and Bennett (2005) cite an example: a girl could not be admitted to a children's ward because her behaviour 'may have been too distressing for other children', nor to an adult ward because of security concerns, and so was admitted to a neonatal ward. This decision caused the girl herself distress. It has been noted that secure and forensic units often admit young people up to the age of 21 (Mears et al., 2003). Specialist units might be particularly difficult in parts of Scotland where the population is sparse and the number of children involved will be very small. The more specialised the unit the greater the distance it is likely to be from the young person's home, with the attendant problems of maintaining or re-establishing family contact and relationships. This was acknowledged by those making representation on behalf of children:

> For many young people with a mental disorder, to be transferred from the Highlands and Islands to Glasgow would be distressing in itself. However, we must balance that with the fact that it may be more distressing to be admitted to an adult ward. (Eddie Follan, Children in Scotland, in Scottish Parliament, 2002g, col. 3313)

Accommodation for families may help some of these problems.

These and other issues were highlighted in a small descriptive study of 11 young people (10 of them girls) (White and Bennett, 2005). Interestingly all were disappointed with outpatient services, believing them 'not intensive enough to meet their needs', and four explicitly stated that they should have been admitted earlier. However, some believed that more appropriate outpatient services would have prevented the need for admission.

Children can be admitted to hospital not just under the MHCT Act but also under the Children Act 1989. They can also be admitted against their will, if their parent(s) consent, without using any legislation: this can give rise to an anomaly whereby a young person with 'Gillick competency' who is able to consent to treatment is then unable to refuse treatment when a parent is able to make a proxy consent for them (Potter and Evans, 2004).

The complexity of the legal issues and psychiatrists' knowledge of the various legislation have been highlighted in England and Wales (Mears and Worrall, 2001; McNamara, 2002; Mears et al., 2003; Potter and Evans, 2004).

Services for women with post-natal depression

Section 24 of the MHCT Act lays out conditions for the 'provision of services and accommodation for certain mothers with post-natal depression'. Essentially this is a requirement to ensure that services and accommodation are in place to allow a woman with parental responsibility for a child aged under one, who 'is not likely to endanger the health or welfare of the child' and 'if she wishes, to care for the child in hospital'. Such units are usually referred to as mother-and-baby units for simplicity.

Although the Act refers specifically to post-natal depression, guidance drawn up by a short-life working group to assist with the planning of such services used the term 'perinatal mental illness' to highlight the wider scope such services might have (and this is the term used in the JLIP delivery indicators). This could include managing the mental health of women with mental illness during their pregnancy. A guidance document was produced by the Scottish Executive in March 2004 (Scottish Executive, 2004d). This was greeted positively by the then Minister for Health and Community Care, Malcolm Chisholm, who said:

> The care and treatment of women who experience mental ill health after they have given birth is of the utmost importance not least for the continuity of the essential bonding between mother and child. (Scottish Executive, 2004e)

The guidelines adopt 'the overarching principle that staff approaches and procedures be designed to enhance and support, wherever possible, the mother as the principal carer for her child'. The 'admission' of the child will, in 'most cases' only be accepted 'if the mother expresses a wish to care for the child in hospital'. A father (who has parental rights) 'may be entitled to remove the child' but has no rights to ask for the child to be taken into hospital.

The development of such services has been slow. Although the Act makes provision for health boards to collaborate with each other 'to whatever extent is necessary to fulfil [their] duty', at the end of 2005 only the West of Scotland Mother and Baby Unit was in existence. Based at the Southern General Hospital in Glasgow, it takes referrals from not only Greater Glasgow and Clyde, but also Ayrshire and Arran, Dumfries and Galloway and Lanarkshire. In addition, it accepts referrals from the Western Isles on a pay per bed usage basis. The unit has six beds and cots, although twins have meant that a maximum of seven babies have been accommodated at one time so far. Although two of the beds are formally for use by health boards outwith Glasgow, bed usage will be on the basis of clinical need so the number of Glasgow and non-Glasgow patients is expected to vary over time. The unit won a nursing award from the Scottish Executive in September 2005, one of five awards and the only one in mental health (Scottish Executive, 2005h).

There are plans for another unit, to be based at St John's Hospital in Livingston, which will serve the east coast health boards, but this will not be available for some time.

Local authority services

Local authorities have a number of duties to provide or secure provision of 'care and support services' (section 25), 'services designed to promote well-being and social development' (section 26) and 'assistance with travel' (section 27).

The aim of such services is to 'minimise the effect of the mental disorder' and to give people 'the opportunity to lead lives which are as normal as possible' (section 25(2)(a-b)). The services to promote well-being and social development include:

(a) social, cultural and recreational activities;

(b) training for such of those persons as are over school age; and

(c) assistance for such of those persons as are over school age in obtaining and in undertaking employment (section 26(2)).

These services are mandatory 'for persons who are not in hospital and who have or have had a mental disorder', and may be provided for people currently in hospital. An explicit example of collaboration is given later for the provision of advocacy (section 259). Several children's groups have noted that this expressly excludes children and that there is an equal, but different, need for prevention services for children, dealing with issues ranging from abuse to bullying (Community Care, 2002a)

In separating the duties of health boards and local authorities, the Act adopts a curiously traditional approach to the provision of services in the light of Joint Future policy, the move to joint commissioning of mental health services, and the community care agenda in general. Concern has been expressed that effort might be wasted in trying to establish who is responsible for the provision of a particular service:

> the possibility of quarrels over who does what – turf wars – when the whole thrust of policy in this area is for services to be provided jointly and for the distinction between what happens in hospital and what happens in the community to be broken down. (Professor Juliet Cheetham, Mental Welfare Commission for Scotland, in Scottish Parliament, 2002b, cols 3058–9)

There is not the space here to detail the types of service provision which will need to be provided or commissioned. As well as working with health boards voluntary organisations will almost certainly play a growing part in providing services, and there may be development of private provision, although this is likely to remain comparatively small. The impact of other related policies in relation to housing (for example tenancy provisions) and benefit payments (including direct payments for provision of services) will continue to influence the type of service development and the method of provision.

Reciprocity

Reciprocity was one of the guiding principles of the Millan Committee (Scottish Executive, 2001a) in its review of the legislation. The definition used by the Scottish Executive is:

> Where society imposes an obligation on an individual to comply with a programme of treatment of care, it should impose a parallel obligation on the health and social services, to provide safe and appropriate services, including ongoing care following discharge from compulsion. (Scottish Executive, 2004a, p. 2)

Previously the most common definition was that given by Eastman (1994) 'that the restriction or removal of civil liberties for the purpose of care must be matched by adequate quality of services'.This is translated into a practice view by an MHO:

> Services have to be delivered in the spirit of reciprocity. So, if a person's liberty is taken away by detention, there must be reciprocal arrangements to improve that person's mental health. These should include support services, the right to advocacy and a statutory adherence to an individual's (and carer's) wishes if they become mentally unwell. Setting up these arrangements promises to be a tough challenge. (Wood, 2005)

Service users' concerns about CB-CTOs were expressed in relation to reciprocity:

> Without reciprocity ... service users feel that compulsory treatment orders in the community will exist in the community will not be a last, but a first resort [sic], and will be used purely to make people take medication – treatment they would refuse in other circumstances. (Keith Maloney, Consultation and Advocacy Promotion Service, in Scottish Parliament, 2002f, col. 3286)

Although there is little dispute about the principle of reciprocity under some general principle of fairness, it is by no means without its problems. Not least is what are, and who defines, adequate or appropriate services, and when 'reciprocity' is seen to apply.

The question of adequate and appropriate services may have been answered to some extent by the number and variety of guidelines published in recent years. These go some way to providing a national or universal standard for service provision and include UK and Scottish-only guidelines. They range from the National Framework (Scottish Office, 1997) and its amendments, to SNAP reports, SIGN guidelines (Scottish Intercollegiate Guidelines Network) and those produced by the Royal College of Psychiatrists or NICE (National Institute for Clinical Excellence). The range covers what services should be available, sets standards for such services, and establishes guidelines for individual treatments and treatment approaches. That these are produced by groups dominated by professionals may be of concern to some. They can be supplemented by assessments of effectiveness of treatments provided by Cochrane reviews.

There are also a range of organisations which have responsibility for monitoring the standards of services, including the Mental Welfare Commission, NHSQIS (NHS Quality Improvement Scotland) and the Social Services Inspectorate. Again, although these have service users and carers involved in inspection teams they are, nevertheless, professionally dominated.

Implicit in the definitions and most discussion on reciprocity is the assumption that the services being prescribed are those received while subject to the Act. The Millan/Scottish Executive definition goes further by including aftercare services. The Act itself does not specify how long such services should be provided for, nor on what basis. This is likely to contribute to different levels of service across the country. The provision for aftercare services is, in itself, important following the ruling in England against Christopher Clunis who tried to sue Camden and Islington Health Authority for not providing appropriate aftercare services. This was described as contributing to his mental decline, which resulted in the death of Jonathon Zito (Franks and Cobb, 2005).

A broader approach to reciprocity can be taken, however, by looking at service provision, care and treatment as a whole. The argument could then be that where provision is made to detain and compulsorily treat patients, the greatest obligation is to provide services and care packages to a level which will keep people, if not always out of hospital, then at least as voluntary patients. The emphasis then would have to be on improving and expanding community emergency and crisis services, and improving inpatient facilities so that people are less reluctant to use them.

Richard Norris, then policy director for SAMH, is reported as saying the 'true test of this bill will be the use of compulsory powers falling, and better community services in place' (Kenny, 2003).

Some service users argue that if they could receive the services they want, rather than those that are on offer, then they would be prepared to engage with services and may thus avoid crises and admissions. Some argue it is less the services themselves but more the attitude of staff which is most at issue.

Given the current approach to a person's right to receive treatment when unable to make that decision for themselves, it is unlikely that a stage would be reached where there is no need for detention at all. How far detention could be reduced is open to question, but the possibility of reducing it through provision of a wider range of services, including crisis beds in small community units, could be examined. Such an examination would need careful analysis of costs and resources, including numbers of (available) staff, set against number and length of admissions and total use of services.

Another issue frequently raised by carers, and by some service users, is the difficulty of getting admission when the person is becoming unwell, wants admission and would accept it. At any meeting of carers, stories are told of people being refused admission 'because they are not ill enough' although both service user and carer, and sometimes the doctor as well, recognise that the person is becoming ill. Pressure on beds is usually given as the reason for non-admission. An example was given to the Health and Community Care Committee:

> A person came to my office last year in crisis. I phoned the services and asked whether he could be admitted but they said there were no beds ... he ended up having to be sectioned a few weeks later ...

A year later, again in crisis, the man wanted to be hospitalised:

> I phoned the services and asked them whether he could be put in hospital ... they came and sectioned him ... I was told that was the only way they could get a bed for him. (Pat Webster, Hearing Voices, in Scottish Parliament, 2002d, cols 3190–1)

Without research, however, it is not possible to know how often this in fact happens, how many people go on to be admitted, either voluntarily or under the Act, and what interventions and community services may cause admission to be unnecessary.

The major concern about reciprocity is, however, essentially one of unintended consequence. While it may be fair to have a particular duty to patients who are being treated compulsorily, where resources are limited this might result in services or treatments being prioritised to patients subject to the Act to the detriment of voluntary patients, resulting in a two-tier system (Atkinson and Patterson, 2000). Swartz and Swanson (2004), commentating from the USA, concluded that outpatient commitment encouraged services to prioritise that group of patients. It would be in no one's interest, particularly patients, if receiving a CTO were a route to accessing scarce resources. While there are anecdotes which suggest that this does happen, again it is only something which monitoring and research will tell us, and in enough detail to act on.

Resources and staffing

For the new MCHT Act to fulfil its potential there is a clear need for adequate resources, which includes appropriate staffing levels, This was made clear by the parliamentary committee reviewing the bill. Margaret Smith MSP, then Chair of the Health and Community Care Committee, is quoted as saying, 'If more money is needed, we would urge the executive to revise the figure. A bill with as many good points as this one deserves to be properly funded' (Community Care, 2002b).

Questions have been raised over the funding for the new service, the adequacy of current services, and the impact on the workforce – particularly psychiatrists, MHOs and advocacy workers. Increased duties and responsibilities for these groups under the Act has led to suggestions that current staff numbers will be insufficient to meet needs and maintain the current service (Atkinson et al., 2002d, 2005; McCollam et al., 2003; Grant, 2004a; Reid, in press). Additional funding is not the answer (or not the whole answer) to this problem as it requires trained staff to be available. Some of the impact was short term. The need to retrain psychiatrists and MHOs in the new Act during 2005 necessarily took people away from their usual duties. This was, however, a one-off necessity, and time for training will revert to the usual levels.

The increased workload is a mixture of additional responsibilities and increased paperwork. For example, MHOs should be consulted by psychiatrists on all detentions, because the option to have a relative consent to an order is no longer available. MHOs also have a responsibility for ensuring that patients are aware of their rights. There is no question that the forms and reports required for applications for orders are considerably longer than under the previous Act. The form to be completed by the MHO for application for a CTO is 27 pages long, and includes detailed questions about care plans and treatment, for perceived future needs as well as current needs. Although many practitioners are commenting negatively on the length of the forms and reports (in private and public if not in print), this is probably to be expected, in part as a response to change. When CCOs were introduced in the Mental Health (Patients in the Community) Act 1995, some psychiatrists complained about the additional bureaucracy for what were perceived as limited powers, although a number later reported that the CCO had proved more useful than they had expected (Atkinson et al., 2000, 2002b). The increased paperwork does add to the workload of already overloaded professionals, and increases the time spent on involuntary patients at the possible expense of voluntary patients (and thus contributes to concerns about a two-tier system).

This has to be balanced against the responsibility of depriving a person of their liberty and requiring them to accept treatment against their will. As a safeguard for both patients and professionals, the reasoning behind this course of action, and the plans for the patient, should be carefully recorded. As with so much of the Act, careful analysis over time should give an indication of the usefulness of this additional work.

Additional money had to be set aside by the Scottish Executive for funding the new Act. Not least were the start-up costs and then running costs of the new MHTS. New services have also been required, including advocacy, perinatal services, age-appropriate services and medium secure units.

Concern has been expressed about what has happened to some of the money allocated to local authorities, for example for advocacy services, as it was not earmarked. Despite this, mental welfare commissioner Juliet Cheetham was reported as saying at a conference in Scotland:

> We do hear that some money for the Act has not reached its destination because it is not actually earmarked funding ... Some money appears to have disappeared into the ether. People need to ask questions about it (Community Care, 2004).

As has been reiterated throughout this book, time will tell. It will take some time for the new Act to bed down and show a clear indication of trends. If it is to be counted a success the impact must be measured across all stakeholder groups.

Useful addresses

British Association of Social Workers (Scotland)
BASW Scotland, Waterloo Place, Edinburgh, EH1 3BG
www.basw.co.uk

Joint Local Implementation Planning (JLIP)
www.show.scot.nhs.uk/mhwbsg/jlip

The Law Society of Scotland
The Law Society of Scotland, 26 Drumsheugh Gardens, Edinburgh, EH3 7YR
www.lawscot.org.uk

Mental Health Tribunal for Scotland
Mental Health Tribunal for Scotland, First Floor, Bothwell House, Hamilton Business Park, Caird Park, Hamilton, M13 0QA
www.mhts.org

Mental Welfare Commission for Scotland
The Mental Welfare Commission, Floor K, Argyle House, 3 Lady Lawson Street, Edinburgh, EH3 9SH
www.mwcscot.org.uk

National Schizophrenia Fellowship (Scotland)
National Schizophrenia Fellowship (Scotland), Claremont House, 130 East Claremont Street, Edinburgh, EH7 4LB
www.nsfscot.org.uk

Royal College of Psychiatrists (Scottish Division)
Royal College of Psychiatrists (Scottish Division), 12 Queen Street, Edinburgh, EH2 1JE
www.rcpsych.ac.uk/college/division/scot

Scottish Association for Mental Health
The Scottish Association for Mental Health, Cumbrae House, 15 Carlton Court, Glasgow, G5 9JP
www.samh.org.uk

Scottish Executive
General enquiries: Scottish Executive, St Andrews House, Regent Road, Edinburgh, EH1 3DG
General website: www.scotland.gov.uk
Law website : www.scotland.gov.uk/About/Departments/LPS

References

Appelbaum, P. (2004) 'Psychiatric advance directives and the treatment of committed patients', *Psychiatric Services*, Vol. 55, pp. 751–63

Atkinson, J. M. (1996) 'The community of strangers: supervision and the new right', *Health and Social Care in the Community*, Vol. 4, pp. 122–5

Atkinson, J. M. (in press) *Advance Directives in Mental Health*, London: Jessica Kingsley

Atkinson, J. M. and Coia D. A. (1989) 'Responsibility to carers – an ethical dilemma', *Psychiatric Bulletin*, Vol. 13, pp. 602–4

Atkinson, J. M. and Coia D. A. (1991) 'Carers, the community and the White Paper', *Psychiatric Bulletin*, Vol. 15, pp. 763–4

Atkinson, J. M. and Coia, D. A. (1995) *Families Coping with Schizophrenia*, Chichester: John Wiley

Atkinson, J. M. and Garner, H. C. (2002) 'Least restrictive alternative: advance statements and the new mental health legislation', *Psychiatric Bulletin*, Vol. 26, pp. 246–7

Atkinson, J. M. and MacPherson, K. (2001) 'Patients' advocacy: the development of a service at the State Hospital, Carstairs, Scotland', *Journal of Mental Health*, Vol. 10, pp. 589–96

Atkinson, J. M. and Patterson, L. E. (2000) *Review of Literature Relating to Mental Health Legislation*, Edinburgh: Central Research Unit, Scottish Executive

Atkinson, J. M., Brown, K., Dyer, J. A. T., Hall, D. J. and Strachan, J. (2002d) *Renewing Mental Health Law. A Scoping Exercise in Respect of the Impact on Psychiatrists' Time*, Edinburgh: Royal College of Psychiatrists, Scottish Division

Atkinson, J. M., Garner, H. C. and Gilmour, W. H. (2004b) 'Models of advance directives in mental health care: stakeholder views', *Social Psychiatry and Psychiatric Epidemiology*, Vol. 39, pp. 673–80

Atkinson, J. M., Garner, H. C., Gilmour, W. H. and Dyer, J. A. T. (2000) 'Views of consultant psychiatrists and mental health officers in Scotland on the Mental Health (Patients in the Community) Act 1995', *Journal of Mental Health*, Vol. 9, pp. 385–95

Atkinson, J. M., Garner, H. C., Gilmour, W. H. and Dyer, J. A. T. (2002a) 'The end of indefinitely renewable leave of absence in Scotland: the impact of the Mental Health (Patients in the Community) Act 1995', *Journal of Forensic Psychiatry*, Vol. 13, pp. 298–314

Atkinson, J. M., Garner, H. C., Gilmour, W. H. and Dyer, J. A. T. (2002b) 'The introduction and evaluation of community care orders following the Mental Health (Patients in the Community) Act 1995', *Journal of Mental Health*, Vol. 11, pp. 417–29

Atkinson, J. M., Garner, H. C., Gilmour, W. H. and Dyer, J. A. T. (2002c) 'Changes to leave of absence in Scotland: the views of patients', *Journal of Forensic Psychiatry*, Vol. 13, pp. 315–28

Atkinson, J. M., Garner, H. C., Gilmour, W. H. and Dyer, J. A. T. (2004a) 'The care programme approach and the end of indefinitely renewable leave of absence in Scotland', *Journal of Mental Health Law*, Vol. 11, pp. 101–10

Atkinson, J. M., Garner, H. C., Patrick, H. and Stuart, S. (2003a) 'Issues in the development of advance directives in mental health care', *Journal of Mental Health*, Vol. 12, pp. 463–74

Atkinson, J. M., Garner, H. C., Stuart, S. and Patrick, H. (2003b) 'The development of potential models of advance directives in mental health care', *Journal of Mental Health*, Vol. 12, pp. 575–84

Atkinson, J. M., Gilmour, W. H., Dyer, J. T., Hutcheson, F and Patterson, L. (1997) 'Consultants' views of leave of absence and community care orders in Scotland', *Psychiatric Bulletin*, Vol. 21, pp. 91–4

Atkinson, J. M., Gilmour, W. H., Dyer, J. T., Hutcheson, F. and Patterson, L. (1998) 'Variation in the use of extended leave of absence in Scottish health boards', *Health Bulletin*, Vol. 56, pp. 871–7

Atkinson, J. M., Gilmour, W. H., Dyer, J. T., Hutcheson, F. and Patterson, L. (1999) 'Retrospective evaluation of leave of absence in Scotland 1988–1994', *Journal of Forensic Psychiatry*, Vol. 10, pp. 131–47

Atkinson, J. M., Reilly J., Garner, H. C. and Patterson, L. (2005) *Review of Literature Relating to Mental Health Legislation*, Edinburgh: Scottish Executive

Backlar, P., McFarland, B. H., Swanson, J. W. and Mahler, J. (2001) 'Consumer, provider, and informal caregiver opinions on psychiatric advance directives', *Administration and Policy in Mental Health*, Vol. 28, pp. 427–41

Bean, A., McGurkin, A. and Macpherson, S. (2000) *An Evaluation of Guardianship under the Mental Health (Scotland) Act 1984*, Edinburgh: Central Research Unit, Scottish Executive

Beech, B. (1999) 'Sign of the times? A 3-day unit of instruction on aggression and violence in health settings for all students during pre-registration nurse training', *Nurse Education Today*, Vol. 19, pp. 610–16

Blofeld, J. (2003) *Independent Inquiry into the Death of David Bennett*, Norfolk, Suffolk and Cambridgeshire Health Authority

Bourgeois, W. (1995) *Persons. What Philosophers Say About You*, Ontario: Wilfred Laurier University Press

British Medical Association (1995) *Advance Statements About Medical Treatment: Code of Practice*, London: British Medical Association

Brown, D. (2002) 'Draft Mental Health Bill receives frosty reception from professionals', *Community Care*, Vol. 1429, pp. 18–19

Brown, J. D. (2003) 'Is involuntary outpatient commitment a remedy for community mental health services failure?', *Ethical Human Sciences and Services*, Vol. 5, pp. 7–20

Caldicott, F. (1994) 'Supervision registers: the College's response', *Psychiatric Bulletin*, Vol. 18, pp. 8

Calton, T. and Arcelus, J. (2003) 'Adolescent units: a need for change?', *Psychiatric Bulletin*, Vol. 27, pp. 292–4

Carter, D. (1999) *The Nearest Relative under the Mental Health Act*, MA thesis. Anglia Polytechnic University

Chadwick, E. (1842) *Report on the Sanitary Conditions of the Labouring Population of Great Britain*, edited Flin, M. W., 1925, Edinburgh: University of Edinburgh Press

Collins, J. (1994) 'Nurses' attitudes towards aggressive behaviour, following attendance at "The Prevention and Management of Aggressive Behviour Programme"', *Journal of Advanced Nursing*, Vol. 20, pp. 117–31

Community Care (2002a) 'Scots bill "excludes children's needs"', *Community Care*, Vol. 1451, p. 12

Community Care (2002b) 'Cash warning for Scottish proposals', *Community Care*, Vol. 1452, p. 11

Community Care (2004) 'Commissioner warns that money for Mental Health Act has "disappeared"', *Community Care*, Vol. 1548, p. 8

Crossley, B. (2004) 'Mental health review tribunals: recent problems', *Psychiatric Bulletin*, Vol. 28, pp. 384

Curie, C. G. (2005) 'SAMHSA's commitment to eliminating the use of seclusion and restraint', *Psychiatric Services*, Vol. 56, pp. 1139–40

Dace, E. A. (2001) 'A cat among the pigeons', *Mental Health Today*, November pp. 29–31

Dawson, J. (2005) *Community Treatment Orders: International Comparisons*, Faculty of Law, University of Otago, New Zealand

Dawson, J. and Romans, S. (2001) 'Uses of community treatment orders in New Zealand: early findings', *Australian and New Zealand Journal of Psychiatry*, Vol. 35, pp. 190–5

Dawson, J., Romans, S., Gibbs, A. and Ratter, N. (2003) 'Ambivalence about community treatment orders', *International Journal of Law and Psychiatry*, Vol. 26, pp. 243–55

Department of Health (1998a) *Modernising Mental Health Services*, London: HMSO

Department of Health (1998b) 'Expert advisor appointed to start review of Mental Health Act', press release 22 September 98/391, London: Department of Health

Department of Health (1999a) *National Framework for Mental Health*, London: HMSO

Department of Health (1999b) *Review of the Mental Health Act 1983* (Richardson Report), London: HMSO

Department of Health (1999c) *Reform of the Mental Health Act 1983: Summary of Consultation Responses*, London: HMSO

Department of Health (2002a) *Draft Mental Health Bill*, London: HMSO

Department of Health (2002b) *Mental Health Review Tribunal Report: April 1999 to March 2001*, London: Department of Health

Department of Health (2004) *Draft Mental Health Bill*, London: HMSO

Department of Health (2005) *Government Response to the Report of the Joint Committee on the Draft Mental Health Bill 2004*, Cm. 6624, London: HMSO

Department of Health (2006) *The Mental Health Bill: Plans to Amend the Mental Health Act 1983. Briefing sheets on key policy areas where changes are proposed* (online). Available from URL: www.dh.gov.uk/PublicationsAndStatistics/Publications/fs/en (accessed 25 May 2006)

Department of Health and Home Office (2000) *Reforming the Mental Health Act 1983* (White Paper), London: HMSO

Dix, D. (1843) *On Behalf of the Insane Poor: Report to the Legislature of Massachusetts of January 1843* (reprinted 1971) New York: Arno Press

Dolan, M., Gibb, R. and Coorey, P. (1999) 'Mental health review tribunals: a survey of Special Hospital patients' opinions', *Journal of Forensic Psychiatry*, Vol. 10, pp. 264–75

Donat, D.C. (2005) 'Encouraging alternatives to seclusion, restraint and reliance on PRN drugs in a public psychiatric hospital', *Psychiatric Services*, Vol. 56, pp. 1105–8

Dyer, C. (2005) 'Government "has ignored" MPs' recommendations on mental health law', *British Medical Journal*, Vol. 331, p. 178

Dyer, C. (2006) Mental Health Bill for England and Wales may be postponed, *British Medical Journal*, Vol. 332, p. 444

Eastman, N. (1994) 'Mental health law: civil liberties and the principle of reciprocity', *British Medical Journal*, Vol. 308, pp. 43–5

Easton, M. (2006) 'The long road to a mental health law' online. Available from URL: news.bbc.co.uk/1/hi/health/4838066.stm (accessed 9 May 2006)

Erickson, S. K. (2005) 'A retrospective examination of outpatient commitment in New York', *Behavioural Sciences and Law*, Vol. 23, pp. 627–45

Fallon, P., Bluglass, R., Edwards, B. and Daniels, G. (1999) *Report of the Committee of Inquiry into the Personality Disorder Unit, Ashworth Special Hospital*, London: Stationery Office

Ferencz, N. and McGuire, J. (2000) 'Mental health review tribunals in the UK: applying a therapeutic jurisprudence perspective', *Court Review*, Spring, pp. 48–52

Fisher, W. A. (2003) 'Elements of successful restraint and seclusion reduction programs and their application in a large, urban, state psychiatric hospital', *Journal of Psychiatric Practice*, Vol. 9, pp. 7–15

Franks, R. A. and Cobb, D. (2005) *Mental Health Act (Care and Treatment) (Scotland) Act 2003*, Edinburgh: W.Green

Freckelton, I. (2003) Mental health review tribunal decision-making: a jurisprudence lens, *Psychiatry, Psychology and Law*, Vol. 10, pp. 44–62

Frueh, B. C., Knapp, R. G., Cusack, K. J., Grubaugh, A. L., Sauvageot, J. A., Cousins, V. C., Yim, E., Robins, C. S., Monnier, J. and Hiers T.G. (2005) 'Patients' reports of traumatic or harmful experiences within the psychiatric setting', *Psychiatric Services*, Vol. 56, pp. 1123–33

Gerbasi, J., Bonnie, R. and Binder, R (2000) 'Resource document on mandatory outpatient commitment', *Journal of the American Academy of Psychiatry and Law*, Vol. 28, pp. 127–44

Gibbs, A., Dawson, J., Ansley, C. and Mullen, R. (2005) 'How patients in New Zealand view community treatment orders', *Journal of Mental Health*, Vol. 14, pp. 357–68

Gibson, A. C. (2000) 'Medical roles in mental health review tribunals', *British Journal of Psychiatry*, Vol. 176, pp. 496–7

Gillen, S. (2004) 'Issue of detention remains a worry after mental health bill is redrawn', *Community Care*, Vol. 1540, pp. 16–17

Giordano, S. (2003) 'Anorexia nervosa and refusal of naso-gastric treatment', *Bioethics*, Vol. 17, pp. 261–78

Glover, R. W. (2005) 'Reducing the use of seclusion and restraint: a NASMHPD priority', *Psychiatric Services*, Vol. 56, pp. 1141–2

Gordon, J. (2004) *A Comparison of the Adults with Incapacity (Scotland) Act 2000 and the Mental Health (Care and Treatment) (Scotland) Act 2003*, Edinburgh: Scottish Executive

Grant, S. (2004a) *National Mental Health Services Assessment: Towards Implementation of the Mental Health (Care and Treatment) (Scotland) Act 2003. Final Report*, Edinburgh: Scottish Executive

Grant, S. (2004b) *National Mental Health Services Assessment: Towards Implementation of the Mental Health (Care and Treatment) (Scotland) Act 2003. Final Report: Quick Read Summary*, Edinburgh: Scottish Executive

Gregor, C. (1999) *An Overlooked Stakeholder? The Views of the Nearest Relative on the Mental Health Act Assessment*, Anglia Polytechnic University and Suffolk Social Services

Griffith, R. (1988) *Community Care. Agenda for Action. A Report to the Secretary of State for Social Services*, London: HMSO

Grisso, T. and Appelbaum, P. S. (1995) 'The MacArthur Treatment Competence Study: III. Abilities of patients to consent to psychiatric and medical treatments', *Law and Human Behaviour*, Vol. 19, pp. 149–74.

Grisso, T. and Appelbaum, P. S. (1996) 'Values and limits of the MacArthur Treatment Competence Study', *Psychology, Public Policy, and Law*, Vol. 2, pp. 167–81.

Grisso, T., Appelbaum, P. S., Mulvey, E. P. and Fletcher, K. (1995) 'The MacArthur Treatment Competence Study: II. Measures of abilities related to competence to consent to treatment', *Law and Human Behaviour*, Vol. 19, pp. 127–48.

Hatfield, B., Bindman, J. and Pinfold, V. (2004) 'Evaluating the use of supervised discharge and guardianship in cases of severe mental illness: a follow-up study', *Journal of Mental Health*, Vol. 13, pp. 197–209

Hayes, D. (2005) 'Difficulties in staffing of tribunals delays Scots Mental Health Act', *Community Care*, Vol. 1557, p. 14

Henderson, C., Flood, C., Leese, M., Thornicroft, G., Sutherby, K. and Szmukler, G. (2004) 'Effect of joint crisis plans on the use of compulsory treatment in psychiatry: single blind randomised controlled trial', *British Medical Journal*, Vol. 329, pp. 136–40

Henderson, G. (2003) *Parens Patrie or Police Power*, Master of Community Care thesis. University of Glasgow

Hewitt, D. (1999) 'Expert opinion: mental health', *Community Care*, Vol. 130, p. 21

Hiday, V. (2003) 'Outpatient commitment: the state of empirical research on its outcomes', *Psychology, Public Policy, and Law*, Vol. 9, pp. 8–32

Hiday, V. A., Swartz, M. S., Swanson, R. B. and Wagner, H. R. (2002) 'The impact of outpatient commitment on victimization of people with severe mental illness', *American Journal of Psychiatry*, Vol. 159, pp. 1403–11

Home Office/Department of Health (1999) *Managing Dangerous People with Severe Personality Disorder: Proposals for Consultation*, London: Home Office

House of Lords and House of Commons Joint Committee on the Draft Mental Health Bill

(2005) *Draft Mental Health Bill. Session 2004–5 Vol 1*, London: Stationery Office

Infantino, J. A. and Musingo, S-Y. (1985) 'Assaults and injuries among staff with and without training in aggression control techniques', *Hospital and Community Psychiatry*, Vol. 36, pp. 1312–4

Jaworowski, S. and Guneva R. (2002) Decision-making in Community Treatment Orders: a comparison of clinicians and Mental Health Board Review members, *Australasian Psychiatry* Vol. 10 pp. 39–32

Jones, K. (1991) 'Law and mental health: stick or carrots?', in Berrios, G. E. and Freeman, H. (eds) (1991) *150 Years of British Psychiatry 1841–1991*, London: Gaskell

Kappler, G. (in press) 'New Act makes immediate impact', *Mental Health Officer Newsletter*

Kenny, C. (2003) 'Scottish shake-up bids to balance interest of the public and clients', *Community Care*, Vol. 1466, pp. 16–17

Kinton, M. (2005) 'Mental health law for the 21st century?', *Journal of Mental Health Law*, Vol. 12, pp. 57–69

Kisley, S., Campbell, L. A. and Preston, N. (2005) 'Compulsory community and involuntary outpatient treatment for people with severe mental disorders', *Cochrane Database of Systematic Reviews* 2005, Art. no.: CD004408, pub. 2, DOI:10.1002/14651856

Kmietowicz, Z. (2002) 'Organisations unite against draft mental health Bill', *British Medical Journal*, Vol. 325, p. 9

Law Commission (1995) *Mental Incapacity. Law Commission No 231*, London: HMSO

Law Society (2005) 'The Law Society's response to the draft Mental Health Bill', *Journal of Mental Health Law*, Vol. 12, pp. 70–6

Lawton-Smith, S. (2005) *A Question of Numbers: The Potential Impact of Community-based Treatment Orders in England and Wales*, London: King's Fund

Leason, K. (2002a) '"Choice not compulsion": opposition grows to draconian health bill', *Community Care*, Vol. 1436, pp. 20–1

Leason, K. (2002b) 'Mental health tsar remains bullish in the face of criticism of draft bill', *Community Care*, Vol. 1442, pp. 18–19

Leason, K., Jobson, A. and Sale, A. V. (2002) 'Mental Health Alliance attacks draft legislation as flawed and unworkable', *Community Care*, Vol. 1440, p. 8

Lee, S., Wright, S., Sayer, J., Parr, A-M., Gray, R. and Gournay, K. (2001) 'Physical restraint training for nurses in English and Welsh psychiatric intensive care and regional secure units', *Journal of Mental Health*, Vol. 10, pp. 151–62

MacAttram, M (2006) 'Bad bill bites dust', The 1990 Trust (online). Available from URL: www.blink.org.uk/pdescription.asp?key=1103&grp+5&cat=293 (accessed 9 May 2006)

McCollam, A., McLean, J., Gordon, J. and Moodie, K. (2003) *Mental Health Officer Services: Structures and Supports*, Edinburgh: Scottish Executive

McKenzie, S. (2005) 'Caught in the crossfire', *Public Health News*, 11 April, p 9

McManus, J. J. and Thomson, L. (2005) *Mental Health and Scots Law in Practice*, Edinburgh: W. Green

McNamara, D. (2002) 'Mental health legislation in child and adolescent psychiatry in England and Wales', *Irish Journal of Psychological Medicine*, Vol. 19, pp. 66–9

Maden, A. (2005) 'The point of principles: commentary on the draft Mental Health Bill in England: without principles', *Psychiatric Bulletin*, Vol. 29, pp. 250–1

Mears, A. and Worrall, A. (2001) 'A survey of psychiatrists' views of the use of the Children Act and the Mental Health Act in children and adolescents with mental health problems', *Psychiatric Bulletin*, Vol. 25, pp. 304–6

Mears, A., White, R. and Lelliott, P. (2003) 'Consultant child and adolescent psychiatrists' knowledge of and attitude to the use of legislation concerning young people with psychiatric disorder', *Psychiatric Bulletin*, Vol. 27, pp. 367–70

Melamed, Y., Mester, R., Margolin, J. and Kalian, M. (2003) 'Involuntary treatment of anorexia nervosa', *International Journal of Law and Psychiatry*, Vol. 26, pp. 617–26

Mental Health Act Commission (1991) *Annual Report*, London: MHAC

Mental Health Officer Newsletter (in press) 'MHO experience of the new Act and tribunals'

Mental Health Tribunal for Scotland (2004a) *Regulations for Appointment of Legal Members*, SSI 2004/286, Edinburgh: Stationery Office

Mental Health Tribunal for Scotland (2004b) *Regulations for Appointment of Medical Members*, SSI 2004/374, Edinburgh: Stationery Office

Mental Health Tribunal for Scotland (2004c) *Regulations for Appointment of General Members*, SSI 2004/375, Edinburgh: Stationery Office

Mental Welfare Commission for Scotland (1996) *Annual Report 1995–1996*, Edinburgh: Mental Welfare Commission for Scotland

Mental Welfare Commission for Scotland (1998) *Restraint of Residents with Mental Impairment in Care Homes and Hospitals*, Edinburgh: Mental Welfare Commission for Scotland

Mental Welfare Commission for Scotland (2004) *Annual Report 2003–2004*, Edinburgh: Mental Welfare Commission for Scotland

Mental Welfare Commission for Scotland (2005a) *Our Annual Report*, Edinburgh: Mental Welfare Commission for Scotland

Mental Welfare Commission for Scotland (2005b) *Guidance on the Admission of Young People to Adult Mental Health Wards*, Edinburgh: Mental Welfare Commission for Scotland

Moncrieff, J. (2003) 'The politics of a new Mental Health Act', *British Journal of Psychiatry*, Vol. 183, pp. 8–9

Mullen, P. E. (2005) 'Facing up to our responsibilities: commentary on the draft Mental Health Bill in England: without principles', *Psychiatric Bulletin*, Vol. 29, pp. 248–9

NICE (2005) *The Short-term Management of Disturbed/Violent Behaviour in Psychiatric Inpatient Settings and Emergency Departments*, London: NICE

Obomanu, W. and Kennedy, H. G. (2001) '"Juridogenic" harm: statutory principles for the new mental health tribunals', *Psychiatric Bulletin*, Vol. 25, pp. 331–3

O'Reilly, R. and Bishop, J. (2001) 'Assessing the New York City involuntary outpatient treatment program', *Psychiatric Services,* 52, p. 1533

Papageorgiou, A., King, M., Janmohamed, A., Davidson, O. and Dawson, J. (2002) 'Advance directives for patients compulsorily admitted to hospital with serious mental illness: randomised controlled trial', *British Journal of Psychiatry*, Vol. 181, pp. 513–19

Papageorgiou, A., Janmohamed, A., King, M., Davidson, O. and Dawson, J. (2004) 'Advance directives for patients compulsorily admitted to hospital with serious mental illness: directives content and feedback from patients and professionals', *Journal of Mental Health*, Vol. 13, pp. 379–88

Parry-Jones, W. Ll. (1972) *The Trade in Lunacy*, London: Routledge

Peay, J. (1989) *Tribunals on Trial: A Study of Decision-making Under the Mental Health Act 1983*, Oxford: Clarendon Press

Peay, J. (2003) *Decisions and Dilemmas. Working with Mental Health Law*, Oxford: Hart Publishing

Peay, J. (2005) 'Decision-making in mental health law: can past experience predict future practice?', *Journal of Mental Health Law*, May, pp. 41–56

Percy Commission (1957) *Report of the Royal Commission on the Law Relating to Mental Illness and Mental Deficiency 1954–1957*, Cmnd 169, London: HMSO

Phillips, D. and Rudestam, K. E. (1995) 'Effect of non-violent self-defence training on male psychiatric staff members' aggression and fear', *Psychiatric Services*, Vol. 46, pp. 164–8

Phin, L. (2005) *Children and Young People's Mental Health: A Framework for Promotion, Prevention and Care: Draft for Consultation. Analysis of Consultation Responses*, Edinburgh: Scottish Executive

Pinfold, V., Bindman, J., Thornicroft, G., Franklin, D. and Hatfield, B. (2001) 'Persuading the persuadable: evaluating compulsory treatment in England using Supervised Discharge Orders', *Social Psychiatry and Psychiatric Epidemiology*, Vol. 36, pp. 260–6

Politics.co.uk (2006) 'Ministers unveil new mental health plans' (online,23 March). Available from URL: www.politics.co.uk/public-services/health/ministers-unveil-new-mental -health-plans-$17076667.htm (accessed 26 May 2006)

Porter, R. (1990) *Mind Forg'd Manacles. A History of Madness in England from the Restoration to the Regency*, London: Penguin

Potter, R. and Evans, N. (2004) 'Child psychiatry, mental disorder and the law: is a more specific statutory framework necessary?', *British Journal of Psychiatry*, Vol. 184, pp. 1–2

Preston, N. J., Kisely, S. and Xiao, J. (2002) 'Assessing the outcome of compulsory psychiatric treatment in the community: epidemiological study in Western Australia', *British Medical Journal*, Vol. 324, p. 1244

Prins, H. A. (2000) 'Complex medical roles in mental health review tribunals', *British Journal of Psychiatry*, Vol. 177, p. 182

Public Health News (2005) 'Sector protests at "hopelessly complex" bill', *Public Health News*, 7 February, p 5

Rapaport, J. (2004) 'A matter of principle: the nearest relative under the Mental Health Act 1983 and proposals for legislative reform', *Journal of Social Welfare and Family Law*, Vol. 26, pp. 377–96

Rapaport, J. (2005) 'The informal caring experience: issues and dilemmas', in Ramon, S. and Williams, J.E. (eds) (2005) *Mental Health at the Crossroads: The Promise of the Professional Approach*, Aldershot: Ashgate

Reid, L. (in press) 'How many MHOs are there and are there enough?', *Mental Health Officer Newsletter*

Richardson, G. (2005) 'Two bills; two agendas', *Journal of Mental Health Law*, Vol. 12, pp. 26–30

Richardson, G. and Machin, D. (2000) 'Doctors on tribunals: a confusion of roles', *British Journal of Psychiatry*, Vol. 176, pp. 110–15

Ridgely, M. S., Borum, R. and Petrila J. (2001) *The Effectiveness of Involuntary Outpatient Treatment: Empirical Evidence and the Experience of Eight States*, Santa Monica CA: RAND Institute for Civil Justice and RAND Health

Robbins, C. S., Sauvageot, J. A., Cusack, K. J., Suffoletta-Maierle, S. and Frueh, B. C. (2005) 'Consumers' perceptions of negative experiences and "sanctuary harm" in psychiatric settings', *Psychiatric Services*, Vol. 56, pp. 1134–8

Ross, M. (2005) 'Whose right is it anyway?', *Newsletter for MHOs in Scotland*, Issue 10, pp. 14, 11

Royal College of Psychiatrists (2002) *Acute In-patient Psychiatric Care for Young People with Severe Mental Illness: Recommendations for Commissioners, Child and Adolescent Psychiatrists and General Psychiatrists. Council Report CR106*, London: Royal College of Psychiatrists

Royal College of Psychiatrists Research Unit (1998) *Management of Immanent Violence: Clinical Practice Guidelines to Support Mental Health Services*, London: Royal College of Psychiatrists

Saks, E. R. (2003) 'Involuntary outpatient commitment', *Psychology, Public Policy, and Law*, Vol. 9, pp. 94–106

Savulescu, J. and Dickenson, D. (1998) 'The time frame preferences, dispositions, and the validity of advance directives for the mentally ill', *Philosophy, Psychiatry and Psychology*, Vol. 5, pp. 225–46

Schopp, R. F. (2003) 'Outpatient civil commitment: a dangerous charade or a component of a comprehensive institution of civil commitment?' *Psychology, Public Policy, and Law*, Vol. 9, pp. 33–69

Scott-Moncrieff, L. (2005) 'A sense of "déjà vu" – a preliminary (and immediate) response to the report of the Scrutiny Committee on the draft Mental Health Bill', *Journal of Mental Health Law*, Vol. 12, pp. 77–82

Scottish Association for Mental Health (2002) Media release, 16 September

Scottish Committee of the Council for Tribunals (2005) *The Annual Report of the Scottish Committee of the Council for Tribunals for the Period 1 April 2004 – 31 March 2005*, Edinburgh:

Scottish Executive
Scottish Executive (2000) *Independent Advocacy: A Guide for Commissioners*, Edinburgh: Scottish Executive
Scottish Executive (2001a) *New Directions: Report on the Review of the Mental Health (Scotland) Act 1984* (Millan Committee), Edinburgh: Scottish Executive
Scottish Executive (2001b) *Renewing Mental Health Law: Policy Statement*, Edinburgh: Scottish Executive
Scottish Executive (2003) *An Introduction to the Mental Health (Care and Treatment) (Scotland) Act 2003*, Edinburgh: Scottish Executive
Scottish Executive (2004a) *The New Mental Health Act: What's It All About? A Short Introduction*, Edinburgh: Scottish Executive
Scottish Executive (2004b) *The New Mental Health Act: A Guide to Advance Statements*, Edinburgh: Scottish Executive
Scottish Executive (2004c) *The New Mental Health Act: A Guide to Named Persons*, Edinburgh: Scottish Executive
Scottish Executive (2004d) *A Framework for Mental Health Services in Scotland: Perinatal Mental Illness/Postnatal Depression Hospital Admission and Support Services*, Edinburgh: Scottish Executive
Scottish Executive (2004e) News release, 4 March, Edinburgh: Scottish Executive
Scottish Executive (2005a) *Mental Health (Care and Treatment) (Scotland) Act 2003 Code of Practice Vol. I*, Edinburgh: Scottish Executive
Scottish Executive (2005b) *The New Mental Health Act: A Guide to Emergency and Short-term Powers. Information for Service Users and Their Carers*, Edinburgh: Scottish Executive
Scottish Executive (2005c) *The New Mental Health Act. A Guide to Compulsory Treatment Orders. Information for Service Users and Their Carers*, Edinburgh: Scottish Executive
Scottish Executive (2005d) *Mental Health (Care and Treatment) (Scotland) Act 2003 Code of Practice Vol. II*, Edinburgh: Scottish Executive
Scottish Executive (2005e) 'Mental Health Tribunal for Scotland', news release, 22 April
Scottish Executive (2005f) *The New Mental Health Act: A Guide to Independent Advocacy. Information for Service Users and Their Carers*, Edinburgh: Scottish Executive
Scottish Executive (2005g) *The Mental Health of Children and Young People: A Framework for Promotion, Prevention and Care*, Edinburgh: Scottish Executive
Scottish Executive (2005h) 'Nurses win award for patient care', news release, 14 September
Scottish Needs Assessment Programme (2003) *Needs Assessment Report on Child and Adolescent Mental Health*, Edinburgh: Public Health Institute for Scotland
Scottish Office (1997) *A Framework for Mental Health Services in Scotland*, Edinburgh: Stationery Office
Scottish Parliament (1999) Mental Health (Public Safety and Appeals) (Scotland) Act, Edinburgh: Stationery Office
Scottish Parliament (2000) Adults with Incapacity (Scotland) Act, Edinburgh: Stationery Office
Scottish Parliament (2002a) *Mental Health (Scotland) Bill*, Edinburgh: Stationery Office
Scottish Parliament (2002b) Health and Community Care Committee Official Report, 25 September
Scottish Parliament (2002c) Health and Community Care Committee Official Report 2 October
Scottish Parliament (2002d) Health and Community Care Committee Official Report 4 October
Scottish Parliament (2002e) Health and Community Care Committee Official Report 9 October
Scottish Parliament (2002f) Health and Community Care Committee Official Report 30 October
Scottish Parliament (2002g) Health and Community Care Committee Official Report 6 November
Scottish Parliament (2003) Mental Health (Care and Treatment) (Scotland) Act, Edinburgh: Stationery Office
Scottish Parliament (2004) *The Mental Health Tribunal for Scotland (Practice and Procedures) Rules: Draft*, Edinburgh: Stationery Office

Scottish Parliament (2005) The Mental Health Tribunal for Scotland (Practice and Procedures) Rules 2005, SSI 2005/420, Edinburgh: Stationery Office

Scull, A. T. (1982) *Museums of Madness. The Social Organisation of Insanity in Nineteenth Century England*, Harmondsworth, Middlesex: Penguin

Shooter, M. and Zigmond, T (2002) *Reform of the Mental Health Act 1983. Letter to College Members*, London: Royal College of Psychiatrists

Shorter, E. (1997) *A History of Psychiatry from the Era of the Asylum to the Age of Prozac*, New York: John Wiley

Smith, G. M., Davis, R. H., Bixler, E. O., Lin, H-N., Altenor, R. J., Hardentstine, B. D. and Kopchick, G. A. (2005) 'Pennsylvania State Hospital System's seclusion and restraint reduction programme', *Psychiatric Services*, Vol. 56, pp. 1115–22

Smith, L. (2006) 'Government scraps mental health bill' (online, 23 March). Available from URL: www.guardian.co.uk/uk_news/story/0,,1738076,00.html (accessed 26 May 2006)

Srebnik, D. and Brodoff, L. (2003) 'Implementing psychiatric advance directives: service provider issues and answers', *Journal of Behavioural Health Services and Research*, Vol. 30, pp. 253–68

Srebnik, D., Appelbaum, P. S. and Russo, J. (2004) 'Assessing competence to complete psychiatric advance directives with the competence assessment tool for advance directives', *Comprehensive Psychiatry*, Vol. 45 pp. 239–45

Srebnik, D. S., Russo, J., Sage, J., Peto, T. and Zick, E. (2003) 'Interest in psychiatric advance directives among high users of crisis services and hospitalization', *Psychiatric Services*, Vol. 54, pp. 981–6

Steadman, H. J., Gounis, K., Dennis, D., Hopper, K., Roche, B., Swartz, M. and Robbins, P. C. (2001a) 'Assessing the New York Involuntary Outpatient Commitment Pilot Program', *Psychiatric Services*, Vol. 52, pp. 330–6

Steadman, H. J., Gounis, K., Dennis, D., Hopper, K., Roche, B., Swartz, M. and Robbins, P. C. (2001b) 'Assessing the New York City Involuntary Outpatient Treatment Programme: In reply', *Psychiatric Services*, Vol. 52, pp. 1533–34

Summers, C., Brown, K., Mackay, K. and Rowlings, C. (2000) *Relatives' Consent Under the Mental Health (Scotland) Act 1984: A Study of Practice, Relatives' Experiences and the Effect on Families, Final Report to the CSO*, University of Stirling

Swain, P. A. (2000) 'Admitted and detained: community members and Mental Health Review Boards', *Psychiatry, Psychology and Law*, Vol. 7, pp. 79–88

Swanson, J. W., Borum, R., Swartz, M. S., Hiday, V. A., Wagner, H. R. and Burns, B. J. (2001) 'Can involuntary outpatient commitment reduce arrests among persons with severe mental illness?', *Criminal Justice and Behaviour*, Vol. 28, pp. 156–89

Swanson, J. W., Swartz, M. S., Borum, R., Hiday, V. A., Wagner, H. R. and Burns, B. J. (2000) 'Involuntary out-patient commitment and reduction of violent behaviour in persons with severe mental illness', *British Journal of Psychiatry*, Vol. 176, pp. 324–31

Swartz, M. S. and Swanson, J. W. (2004) 'Involuntary outpatient commitment, community treatment orders and associated outpatient treatment: what's in the data?', *Canadian Journal of Psychiatry*, Vol. 49, pp. 585–91

Swartz, M. S., Swanson, J.W. and Monahan, J. (2003) 'Endorsement of personal benefit of outpatient commitment among persons with severe mental illness', *Psychology, Public Policy, and Law*, Vol. 9, pp. 70–93

Swartz, M. S., Swanson, J. W., Hiday, V. A., Wagner, H. R., Burns, B. J. and Borum, R. (2001a) 'A randomised controlled trial of outpatient commitment in North Carolina', *Psychiatric Services*, Vol. 52, pp. 325–9

Swartz, M. S., Swanson, J. W., Wagner, H. R., Burns, B. J. and Hiday, V. A. (2001b) 'The effects of involuntary outpatient commitment and depot antipsychotics on treatment adherence in people with severe mental illness', *Journal of Nervous & Mental Disease*, Vol. 189, pp. 583–92

Swartz, M. S., Swanson J. W., Wagner H. R., Hannon M. J., Burns B. J. and Shumway, M. (2003)

'Assessment of four stakeholder groups' preferences concerning outpatient commitment for persons with schizophrenia', *American Journal of Psychiatry*, Vol. 160, pp. 1139–46

Szmukler, G. and Holloway, F. (1998) 'Mental health legislation is now a harmful anachronism', *Psychiatric Bulletin*, Vol. 22, pp. 662–5

Szmukler, G. and Hotopf, M. (2001) 'Effectiveness of involuntary outpatient commitment', *American Journal of Psychiatry*, Vol. 158, pp. 635–54

Tan, J., Hope, T. and Stewart, A. (2003a) 'Competence to refuse treatment in anorexia nervosa', *International Journal of Law and Psychiatry*, Vol. 26, pp. 697–707

Tan, J., Hope, T. and Stewart, A. (2003b) 'Anorexia nervosa and personal identity: the accounts of patients and their parents', *International Journal of Law and Psychiatry*, Vol. 26, pp. 533–48

Tan, J., Hope, T., Stewart, A. and Fitzpatrick, R. (2003c) 'Control and compulsory treatment in anorexia nervosa: the views of patients and parents', *International Journal of Law and Psychiatry*, Vol. 26, pp. 627–45

Taylor, J. and Idris, K. (2003) 'Use of the Mental Health (Scotland) Act (1984) in south Glasgow', *Psychiatric Bulletin*, Vol. 27, pp. 141–4

Taylor, J., Lawrie, S. and Geddes, J. (1996) 'Factors associated with admission to hospital following emergency psychiatric assessment', *Health Bulletin*, Vol. 54, pp. 467–73

Taylor, P. J., Goldberg, E., Leese, M., Butwell, M. and Reed, A. (1999) 'Limits to the value of mental health review tribunals for offender patients: suggestions for reform', *British Journal of Psychiatry*, Vol. 174, pp. 164–9

Thornicroft, G. and Szmukler, G. (2005) 'The Draft Mental Health Bill in England: without principles', *Psychiatric Bulletin*, Vol. 184, pp. 244–7

Turner, C. (2005) 'Seen to be fair?', *The Journal Magazine: The Journal of the Law Society of Scotland*, 24 November

Wagner, H., Swartz, M., Swanson, J., Burns, B. (2003) 'Does involuntary outpatient commitment lead to more intensive treatments?', *Psychology, Public Health and the Law*, Vol. 9, pp. 145–56

Webster, P., Schmidt, U. and Treasure, J. (2003) '"Reforming the Mental Health Act": implications of the Government's white paper for the management of patients with eating disorders', *Psychiatric Bulletin*, Vol. 27, pp. 364–6

White, J., Bennett, F. (2005) *Consulting Children and Young People Who Have Been Admitted to Child and Adolescent Mental Health In-patient Units: A Report for the Mental Welfare Commission for Scotland*, Edinburgh: Scottish Development Centre

Wong, J. G. and Clare, I. C. H. (1999) 'Capacity to make health care decisions: its importance in clinical practice', *Psychological Medicine*, Vol. 29, pp. 437–46

Wood, J. (1999) 'Control and compassion: the uncertain role of mental health review tribunals in the management of the mentally ill', in Webb, D. and Harris, R. (eds) (1999) *Mentally Disordered Offenders: Managing People Nobody Owns*, London: Routledge Taylor and Francis

Wood, M. (2005) 'Alarm bells sound in Scotland at wider mental health role'. *Community Care*, Vol. 1565, pp. 49

Woodcock, A. (1998) 'Pam look-alike's horror as stalker is freed', *The Mirror*, 22 August, p. 23

Index